Qasr Ibrim House 1037

Resurrecting an Excavation

Graham Connah
David Pearson

BAR International Series 2821

2016

Published in 2016 by
BAR Publishing, Oxford

BAR International Series 2821

Qasr Ibrim House 1037

ISBN 978 1 4073 1560 7

BAR
PUBLISHING

BAR titles are available from:

BAR Publishing
122 Banbury Rd, Oxford, OX2 7BP, UK
EMAIL   info@barpublishing.com
PHONE   +44 (0)1865 310431
FAX   +44 (0)1865 316916
www.barpublishing.com

In memory of John Alexander
Project Director at Qasr Ibrim

Acknowledgements

With work that has taken so long, there are inevitably many people who have assisted, some of them no longer alive and others now of unknown location. Based on a 1986 excavation, several of the original field team have nevertheless been of assistance over the years, among them John Alexander, Pamela Rose, Peter French, Tony Bonner, Lawrence Smith, and Nettie Adams. We are also indebted to Peter Rowley-Conwy, who encouraged us to persist with this publication. In addition, we acknowledge the assistance gained from the numerous publications by Bill Adams about Qasr Ibrim, although he was not present on the site in 1986. However, Nettie Adams was present and we are grateful not only for her analysis of the textiles from Site 1037 but also for her extensive work on textiles from Qasr Ibrim sites generally.

More immediately, we owe thanks to Ulla Mannering, in Leiden, The Netherlands, for a copy of paper difficult to access. Similarly, Amanda Brady of the Sudan Archaeological Research Society at the British Museum kindly sent us a copy of another paper. The National Library of Australia also helped by obtaining publications from other libraries in Australia and overseas; Deanna Cronk, Document Supply Officer, was most helpful, as also was Paul Koerbin. We are also especially grateful to Andrew Stawowczyk Long and Sam Cooper; in Andrew's case for digital manipulation of the illustrations, and in Sam's case for digital scanning of image drafts. In addition, during our work on the book we benefitted from the advice of Derek Welsby.

The 1986 excavation of House 1037 at Qasr Ibrim was sponsored by the Egypt Exploration Society of London but funded by a grant to GC from the Australian Research Council, which also contributed to other costs of the 1986 project. In addition, the University of New England, Armidale, New South Wales, provided financial and logistical assistance, and access to library facilities through the Australian National University has been important.

Most of the artefacts excavated from Site 1037, and perhaps some of the ecofacts, were assigned to the Cairo Museum but might subsequently have been moved to the Aswan Museum. A small number of items could have reached the British Museum in London, from the Egypt Exploration Society, but a search of the British Museum collection online (accessed 25.3.16) has revealed only one, an iron pin, 7.6cm long, Museum number EA81062, Registration Number 2008, 1008.987, Excavation number ('Day Number' in this book) 85.12.26/35A. It is entered on an Artefact Index Card, of which GC has a copy, as unstratified from Locus 4, and is therefore not included in the list of artefacts given in this book. A sample of plain potsherds from Qasr Ibrim was also deposited in the Antiquities Museum at the University of New England.

Finally, we wish to emphasize that in writing the book we made use of all the relevant field notes, drawings and photographs in our possession or which we were able to access from the Qasr Ibrim archive now at the British Museum. In particular, we are grateful to Mark Horton who provided copies of photographs from the Archive in 1991.

Contents

List of Figures

List of Tables

x

Abstract

Qasr Ibrim, situated in southern Egypt, is one of the most important archaeological sites of the last two millennia in Africa and is relevant beyond the continent. A major urban site in Nubia, it is situated on a rocky crag above the River Nile. It is well known for its remarkable preservation of organic evidence during an occupation in excess of two thousand years; preservation brought about by the virtually rainless conditions of the site's location. Nevertheless, the creation of Lake Nasser by the construction of the Aswan High Dam has been progressively destroying the site and its contents during recent times. Consequently, the Egypt Exploration Society of London has sponsored excavations spread over more than four decades and a considerable amount of published material has resulted. This book is a further contribution to the record of excavation at this site, although in this case it was done long ago in 1985–1986, funded by the Australian Research Council. As such, it is a study of how much data can be reconstructed from the records of an unpublished excavation, and it presents an opportunity to consider the resulting information in the context of the whole site and that of archaeology in Africa overall. It is a resurrection of an otherwise forgotten investigation, a task that has occupied the authors for over three years and highlighted the problems of undertaking such work after such a long delay. With the passage of time since the excavation, the book also provides an opportunity to review the excavation strategies employed over the years and to reconsider the sequence of material cultural assemblages that have often characterized interpretations of the excavated evidence at this site. Residential continuity rather than cultural succession is indicated by this analysis of old work.

Introduction

Long ago the exemplary excavator and publisher Pitt Rivers (1898: 28) famously stated that, 'A discovery dates only from the time of the record of it, and not from the time of its being found in the soil'. More trenchantly, White (1983: 171) insisted, 'Research which is not available for others to use does not exist … If you do not write it down it does not exist. The converse is also true: what you report and publish is all that exists.' Nevertheless, in spite of such warnings, archaeologists have often been responsible for unpublished work. The subject is littered with unpublished excavations and so-called 'preliminary' publications that were never followed by the promised comprehensive study. Only relatively rarely is such work rescued in later years, a remarkable example from the part of Africa with which this book is concerned being the publication by Török (1997) of John Garstang's excavations at Meroë (Garstang *et al.* 1911), over eighty years after they were carried out. There have been archaeologists who have died before they have published all their excavations and fieldwork and essential records have sometimes been lost in fires, floods, or even wars. The late Thurstan Shaw was perhaps unique in being able to claim that he had published all the excavations that he had ever done but then he did live for almost a hundred years. Most other archaeologists would have unpublished excavations lingering from some part of their career, work that is unpublishable in the opinion of some because it has been superseded by subsequent research. However, given the advantages of the Internet, it could be made available in digital form so as to be available to others. The problem is that the necessary preparation still needs analysis and writing, just as publication on paper requires. The alternative is to dump undigested data into web sites, hoping that someone else will eventually make sense of it. The danger is that such material will be soon forgotten and, given the problems of digital archiving, might not be readily accessible in the future.

Failure to publish can be attributed to several factors. First, excavation is still a major occupation of many archaeologists but there is a tendency to move on to the next site before the publication of a previous one is completed or even started. For academic archaeologists, frequent excavations are expected: colleagues in other disciplines often ask: 'So what are you digging up this year?' For commercial archaeologists, there is the necessity to commence work on the next commission, sometimes before an adequate report has been completed or released about a previous one. Thus, quite quickly, the excavator can drown in incomplete work, as project after project piles up and earlier ones are perforce neglected. The excavation of a new site, that promises important results, will tend to demand priority. Consequently it becomes increasingly difficult to produce a publication soon after an excavation, as Flinders Petrie was able to do in earlier times with his no less than ninety-seven books. Archaeologists have careers to attend to, in which many other activities can demand their time. Students have to be taught, postgraduates supervised, museums administered, heritage bureaucracies dealt with, consultancies completed and so on; it can be difficult to find the time for excavation let alone its publication.

A second reason for failure to publish excavations or for very delayed publication is the great expansion in the range and variety of archaeological evidence over the last few decades. The complexity of this evidence and its specialist analysis, often both expensive of time and money, makes publication increasingly difficult. The preparation of a specialist excavation monograph becomes a major task, which can sometimes take years to complete and then prove difficult to publish.

A third reason for non-existent or inadequate publication is that the greater part of excavation, particularly in developed countries, is now in the form of commercial rather than academic archaeology. The purpose of much of it is to rescue data that would otherwise be destroyed by developments, such as building, road construction, mining and so on. In the opinion of some archaeologists, such work does not need to be published in the conventional manner because it is often bulky, descriptive, and generated by practical demands rather than research questions. Instead it can be made available on a data base, as already mentioned. As such, it has often added significantly to our knowledge of the archaeological past, but sometimes it has not.

As a result of the problems with the publication of excavations, even modern excavators with the best of intentions can take many years to publish their work. Witness the case of the British prehistoric site of Snail Down, excavated in the 1950s but published half a century later (Thomas 2005). Few of us are guiltless in this matter. In the case of a 1986 excavation at Qasr Ibrim, which is the subject of this book, the excavator (GC) moved on to other projects in Uganda (Connah 1996) and in Australia (Connah 2007); his work at Qasr Ibrim was simply left behind. Its neglect was also the consequence of giving priority to several books of synthesis (including Connah 1987, 1988, 1998, 2001, 2004, 2010, 2016) and numerous journal papers on a variety of subjects. It has been a case of publication preventing publication. Eventually, it became essential to try to rescue the 1986 excavation, a daunting task to which a colleague who was not present in the field (DP) has made major contributions, particularly in the ordering and analysis of data. In the process it has been necessary to deal with many problems that have resulted from the delay of thirty years, including the absence or unavailability of some material and records. It has also been necessary to accept the accessible records at face value within the context of the time that they were made, rather than confusing matters by attempting to update them. The result is a book that is as much a study of the consequences of delayed publication, as it is a study of the excavation itself; it is literally an attempt to resurrect it. This has taken several years to achieve and the task has grown as we proceeded, compounded by our Australian location in the world, with limited access to excavation records now archived in London at the British Museum. At first we thought that a substantial journal paper would be an adequate medium of publication but the material proved too much for the necessary compression. Therefore, we have presented our study as a modest book, although some might doubt the value of such an old investigation. However, a project involving seven weeks in the Nubian Desert, necessitating skill, labour, finance, and support from the overall project team, as well as resulting in a diminution of the archaeological resource, did not deserve to be written off as if it had never happened. This, indeed, is what seems to have been necessary for part of the work done in 'the all-important 1978 season', where some of the field records are unavailable and presumably were never published (Adams and Adams 2010: 5; see also Anderson and Adams 1979). So, the following presents both a chronicle of the excavation and an analysis of its findings, taking into account the inevitable weaknesses caused by the passage of so many years since it was conducted. It makes one wonder just how many excavations in various parts of the world have now been forgotten, because they were never published. It is most unlikely that we will ever know.

The Historical Context of the 1985–1986 Qasr Ibrim
Excavation

This book is concerned with the excavation in 1985–1986 of Site 1037H, a house complex in Area 4 at the Nubian urban site of Qasr Ibrim (Fig. 1) For brevity, its excavation is generally referred to in this study as taking place in 1986, because most of the work was done in January and early February of that year. One of us (GC) was the excavator, and

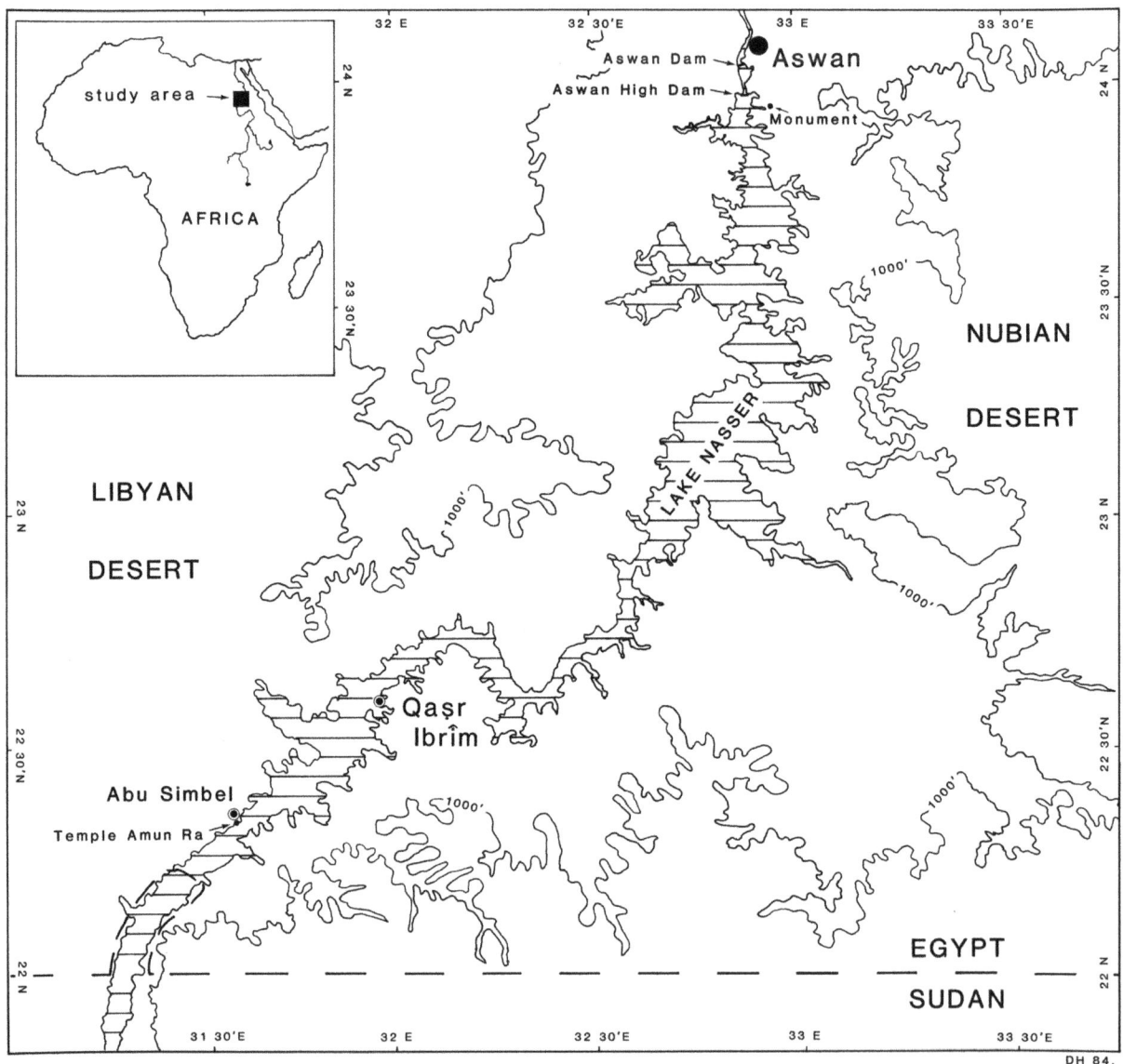

Fig. 1. Southern Egypt showing the location of Qasr Ibrim in relation to Lake Nasser and the surrounding deserts. Drawn by Douglas Hobbs.

was particularly interested in investigating the so-called X-Group in an urban context. The other (DP) has collaborated in the task of understanding the documentation and photographs from thirty years ago, although he was not present at the excavation. Our main purpose in the book is therefore to meet the excavator's obligation to provide an account of the work that was undertaken. As such, the book is more relevant in an historical context than to current field research, which has inevitably moved on in the years since 1986. However, a second purpose of the book is to show the stratigraphic complexity of the excavated structure, that was revealed at a time when *previous* excavation at the site of Qasr Ibrim had sometimes stressed the recovery of structural plans rather than investigation in depth. The 1986 excavation investigated a long series of occupation levels and building periods that had been underwater for a decade. Site 1037H and adjacent areas 1108W, 1109/0 and 1110N produced evidence dating from Napatan to Islamic times, although the latter three areas, to the west of 1037H, had only shallow deposits that are not considered in detail in this book. The majority of the deposits excavated on Site 1037H belonged to Meroitic, X-Group and Early Christian dates and gave an opportunity to examine cultural continuity, particularly with regard to the X-Group. For this reason, in general, excavation was not pursued into deposits earlier than the Meroitic. Deposits later than the Early Christian had rarely survived, due to the destruction of superficial layers and features by the Lake when it covered this area. It should be noted that for convenience, Site 1037H (referred to below as 'Site 1037' or as just '1037') was treated as oriented north–south in the excavation records, but in reality was oriented north–west to south–east (see Fig. 12). However, the orientations of features mentioned in the text and shown in the illustrations are given more specifically wherever possible.

The overall cultural sequence for Lower Nubia, the location of Qasr Ibrim, has been established for many years (Adams 1977; 1982; 1984; 1993; 1996; Ruffini 2012; Adams 2013), at first from cemeteries rather than from occupation sites. The construction of the Aswan High Dam during the 1960s, and the consequent archaeological investigations that took place before the flooding of Lake Nasser, to some extent addressed this problem by the excavation of many different settlements. One major site that at first escaped total inundation was the city of Qasr Ibrim, perched high above the River Nile in a part of its valley where rain is virtually unknown and temperatures are frequently high. As a result of its location, there had been maximum preservation of a wide range of organic materials, which were threatened by the rising Lake. Because of this, excavations that generated a considerable amount of publication were conducted there from 1963 onwards, both in advance of the rising water and subsequently after some of the deposits had been periodically under water (Fig. 2). As time has passed, fluctuating lake levels have been causing further damage to the site and its artefacts, at its maximum the Lake inundating approximately two-thirds of the site (Adams and Adams 2013: 10), although there has been some continued excavation in spite of these problems (Rose 1998; 2000; 2011; Horton 1991). It is therefore particularly important that archaeological evidence from earlier work such as that at Site 1037 be adequately published. The lack of such a publication has

Fig. 2. Qasr Ibrim in 1986 from the south-east. The prominent building in the middle of the site is the Christian Cathedral. Site 1037 is around the corner to the right. At this time the level of Lake Nasser was lower than it had been for some years during the 1970s. Photograph by Graham Connah.

caused some understandable confusion, as in Rose (2011) where Plate 6 on Page 3 shows House 1037 in the foreground and describes it in the text as 'a late Kushite house', although it cannot be identified on the plan of Qasr Ibrim on Page 1 of that paper. Its excavation is attributed to Mark Horton's period of direction from 1988 onwards, not to John Alexander's in 1986, nor is GC mentioned as its excavator. Similarly, Adams and Adams (2013: 10) refer to excavations at Qasr Ibrim after 1982 by Alexander and Driskell, apparently including the 1986 season but again not mentioning the excavation discussed in this book. Adams and Adams (2013) list artefacts excavated from Site 1037 in 1986, as also do Adams and Adams (2010). This information appears to have been obtained from the Artefact Index Cards written on site during the 1986 excavation and subsequently accessed amongst the Qasr Ibrim archives, now kept at the British Museum in London. The excavator of Site 1037 was not consulted on the inclusion of this data from his site. Furthermore, Alexander (1988) refers to a paper by Alexander, Driskell and Connah that is described as 'in press' but was never actually published; so it is as if the 1986 excavation of Site 1037 never happened.

A further justification for the present book is the complexity of the overall Qasr Ibrim site, a city that was occupied at least from the Napatan period, in the early first millennium BC, to the early nineteenth century AD (1812), with significant structural phases of Roman, Meroitic, X-Group, Early Christian, Classic Christian, Late Christian, and Islamic date. Such complexity raised questions regarding the most suitable excavation strategy; how was a large occupation site of this kind to be tackled? According to Adams and Adams (2010: 1, 4): 'The earliest seasons … were characterized by … very deep trenches … which uncovered and at times destroyed the remains of many different periods'. Then from 1972 to 1976 work 'concentrated on the complete clearance of townsite remains of the Ballaña ("X-Group") period'. After 1978 it was hoped to change to a 'level-by-level excavation strategy … exposing and mapping all the remains of each separate level before proceeding downward to the next' but this 'did not work out in practice'. The basic reason was 'a very irregular and almost chaotic stratigraphy' (W.Y. Adams 1996: 12), amongst deposits that have three main components: 'the standing remains of buildings, the fallen or displaced remains of buildings, and the midden (refuse) deposit that accumulated within and around the buildings' (W.Y. Adams 1996: 8). As a consequence: 'There is a problem not only in dating houses, but even in dating individual rooms and floor surfaces within them.'… 'In the upshot, every deposit not only in every house but in every room must be dated independently' (W.Y. Adams 2013: 47). Indeed, in 1986, this was how the 1037 excavation was conducted. Nevertheless, previous excavation at Qasr Ibrim had continued to favour broad areal investigation of the site's major phases (Fig. 3), although also assessing the complexity of individual structures (Adams and Adams 2013). Horton (1990: 487) remarked: 'At Ibrim, it was the intention to excavate the entire site, one index cluster at a time, thus limiting understanding of local stratigraphic sequences or the significance of buildings'. Indeed, Hammond (1990: 471) commented that Horton found W.Y. Adams's

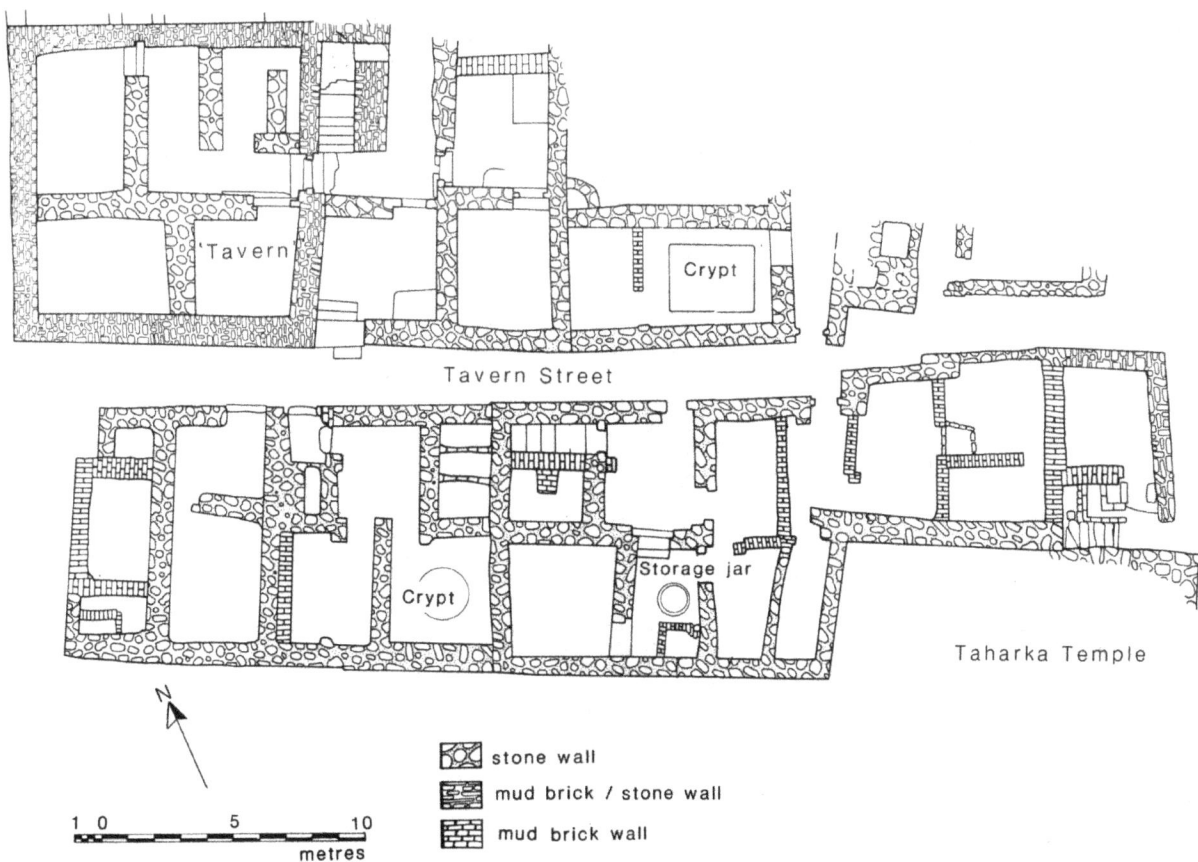

Fig. 3. An example of areal stripping at Qasr Ibrim: plan of 'X-Group' houses beside a narrow street. After Alexander (1988: Fig. 7).

ceramic typology 'flawed by inadequate perception of site formation processes'. Excavation strategies at Qasr Ibrim have since changed but during the 1985–1986 season, when Site 1037 was excavated, it was in the above context that one of us (GC) excavated a house thought to be of the Ballaña Culture (formerly the 'X-Group', Reisner 1910; although the term 'X-Group' was retained by Adams and Adams 2013: 9 'as a type designation for certain pottery types … because it is so thoroughly embedded in the literature'). This house had been partly uncovered during the excavation season of 1983–1984 by Alexander. During that of 1985–1986 it was subjected to detailed stratigraphic excavation, revealing apparent residential continuity in spite of what are considered major cultural changes. The study in this book is essentially historical, presenting the evidence for this conclusion, suggesting that structures at Qasr Ibrim are more complex than the areal stripping of structural phases previously revealed. Perhaps the results of this excavation even question the significance of the cultural labels that have been used at this site. Can an excavator expect to find such a thing as a specifically Meroitic or Ballaña or Early Christian house on an urban site of such limited size but great complexity that was occupied so continuously?

3

The 1985–1986 Excavation

The excavation of Site 1037 took place from 21 December 1985 to 11 February 1986, working six days a week from 6.00 AM to 9.00 AM and 9.30 AM to 1.30 PM, including Christmas Day. In addition, the excavator (GC) was occupied in the afternoons with on-site recording, without the presence of his labour force. Fridays were rest days, in accord with Islamic practice. These details are provided to establish the practical circumstances in which the work took place, as is essential for any experimental procedure. The excavation was an integral part of the then-biennial field seasons conducted at Qasr Ibrim under the auspices of the Egypt Exploration Society of London, with the permission of the Egyptian Antiquities Service. The Australian Research Council provided the funding for the 1037 excavation and also contributed to the overall costs of other work during the 1985–1986 Qasr Ibrim season. The Project Director was John Alexander of St Johns College, Cambridge, who headed a team of fifteen people, including two site archaeologists, Boyce Driskell and Graham Connah, who worked independently. The rest of the team consisted of: a site recorder, pottery analyst, textile analyst, botanical/zoological analyst, leather analyst/assistant recorder, surveyor, photographer, domestic bursar, medical doctor, artist/analysis assistant, and two inspectors from the Egyptian Antiquities Service (Fig. 4). Further details of the team as recorded by the Project Director at the time were as follows:

J. Alexander, B. Driskell, G. Connah: Field archaeologists

P. Rowley-Conwy: Bioarchaeologist

P. French: Registrar [Site Recorder]

N. Adams: Textile analyst

P. Rose: Ceramic analyst

C. Caley: Leather analyst

A. Bonner: Photographer

L. Smith: Surveyor

M. Kausova: Medical Officer

D. Driskell: Domestic Bursar

D. Kusan: Site Assistant

Abd el Hakeem Karar: Antiquities Inspector (Pharaonic)

Magdi Abdeen: Antiquities Inspector (Islamic)

Fig. 4. The excavation team at Qasr Ibrim, 1986. Photograph by Tony Bonner, who is in the front row at the extreme right.

On-site accommodation was provided by the Egyptian government vessel *Gerf Hussein*, which was moored alongside Qasr Ibrim, having been towed up Lake Nasser from Aswan. The *Gerf Hussein* also provided a workroom in which excavation analysis and recording was done (Figs 5 and 6). Furthermore, its open top deck could be used for pottery analysis, which needed a considerable amount of space because of the large quantities, mainly of sherds, that were excavated each day (Fig. 7). The labour force consisted of 32 men from the southern Egyptian town of Quft, which has had a long tradition of providing excavation workers. They were supervised by Reis Bashear who, according to Alexander, had acted in that capacity at Qasr Ibrim for many years. The workmen were divided between the three excavation areas, directed respectively by Alexander, Driskell, and Connah (Fig. 8). Driskell's work uncovered a previously unknown temple probably dating from the eighth century BC to the sixth century AD (Driskell *et al.* 1989); this has been published in some detail, although described as a 'preliminary report'. Alexander excavated various structures and features at the northern end of the peninsula on which Qasr Ibrim stands, including a rock-cut tomb recorded as Grave 1105 (Alexander 1999). The latter publication contains a reference to Alexander (1987), described as '*The 1986 Excavations at Qasr Ibrim.* Unpublished Report, E.E.S. Qasr Ibrim Archive.' Alexander sent a copy of this to GC on 7 July 1986 that has been used in the preparation of this book and was described as a 'preliminary report'. An unpublished typescript by GC that was revised to 31 October 1986 (Connah 1986a) was intended to form part of the paper by Alexander, Driskell and Connah referred to above (see Page 6), and described as 'in press' in

Fig. 5. The *Gerf Hussein* moored at Qasr Ibrim, 3 January 1986. It provided accommodation and workspace for the supervisors and analysts of the excavation team. The excavation labour force lived on the *Abouda*, the vessel to the right. Photograph by Graham Connah.

Fig. 6. The excavation workroom onboard the *Gerf Hussein* in 1986. To the right the Project Director, John Alezander, to the left the excavation recorder, Peter French. Photograph by Graham Connah.

Fig. 7. Baskets of sherds on the top deck of the *Gerf Hussein*, 24 January 1986, awaiting analysis. With three excavations in progress at the same time, Qasr Ibrim produced this quantity of pottery almost every day. After recording, significant material was retained but the remainder was dumped into Lake Nasser. It was impractical to transport all of it to Aswan or Cairo. Photograph by Graham Connah.

Fig. 8. Three of the 1037-site workmen at Qasr Ibrim, 1986. They are in their best clothes, probably on a Friday rest day. Photograph by Graham Connah.

Alexander 1988 but not actually published. For unknown reasons, its preparation was never completed. At the close of the 1037 excavation a handwritten report was also submitted to the Egyptian Antiquities Service by GC that was not intended for publication (Connah 1986b).

Site 1037 was located in 'Area 4', on the 'Southeast Terrace' of the Qasr Ibrim site (Alexander 1987), in an area that was covered by the waters of Lake Nasser for some years during the 1970s but was dry land again by the mid 1980s (Figs 9–11). As a consequence of the submergence of the lower parts of Qasr Ibrim, many structures exposed to the water had disintegrated by January 1984 when GC first saw the site during a three-day initial inspection. During the 1986 excavation, Site 1037 remained adjacent to the lake, on a narrow shelf above which, uphill to its west, there rose a large spoil-dump of rubble and sand from a previous excavation, probably by Plumley in the 1960s. Most of the first nine days of the 1986 excavation was spent cutting back this spoil-dump and removing backfill placed on the 1037 site for protection after its partial exposure in 1984. The latter was by Alexander (1984a; 1984b) and had uncovered the top of surviving structures and included the excavation of one test-pit. It had also uncovered a sandstone lintel inscribed in Meroitic (see Fig. 47). Usually beneath the old spoil-dump material, a thin layer of clean sand and waterworn sherds lay over the undisturbed archaeological features, in effect beach deposits from the Lake during periods when it was at a higher level.

The 1986 excavation of 1037 was basically by trowel and brush, with hoes being used only for the removal of already-loosened deposit or for the excavation of homogeneous

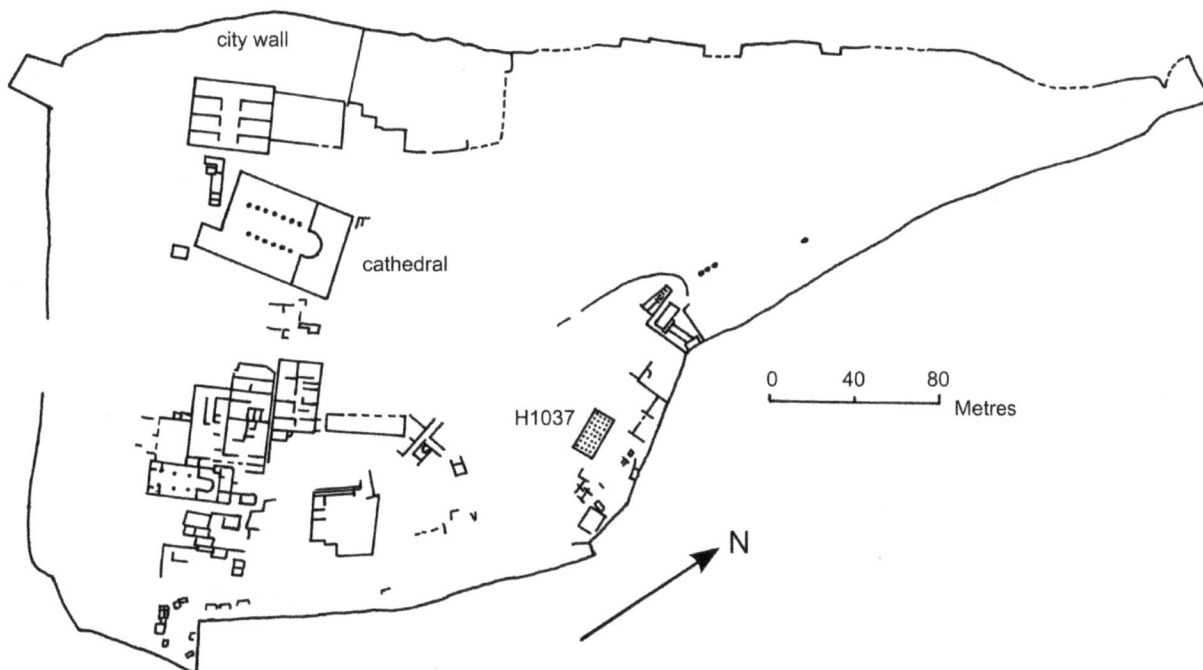

Fig. 9. Plan of Qasr Ibrim showing the location of House 1037 in relation to 'X-Group' structures known at the beginning of the 1985–1986 excavation season. The cathedral and city wall, of different dates, are also shown. After an unpublished draft by Lawrence Smith, redrawn by Graham Connah. Scale is approximate.

Fig. 10. Site 1037 from the north-east, showing the revetment wall (city wall) and the completed excavation on 7 February 1986. Excavated spoil had been dumped over the revetment wall. Photograph by Graham Connah.

Fig. 11. Site 1037 from the north-west, Loci 3 and 10 in the foreground, 6 February 1986. Scale in 10-cm divisions. Photograph by Tony Bonner.

fill that had little intra-fill variation, or for the digging of test-pits. Excavated spoil was not comprehensively sieved; baskets were used for general deposit removal. During excavation, all movable archaeological materials were retained, being separated into analytical subsections of potsherds, bones, botanical remains, textiles, basketry, and small finds (objects of intrinsic significance in themselves). The quantity of pottery was so great that, after analysis and recording, most of the potsherds were discarded by dumping them into the Lake, only intact pots and the more significant sherds being retained. Non-movable evidence (such as walls and floors) were selectively photographed, planned, recorded in two cross-sections, detailed in nearly 20 pages of stratigraphic analysis, and formed the subject of 241 pages of on-site day-to-day field notes (Connah 1986c). Significant masonry items, sometimes recycled, were removed from the site and collected in the 'stone magazine', a storage area near the cathedral (Connah 1986c: 5, 20). In addition, the project analysts compiled detailed records of their examination of the materials submitted to them, some of their reports being included in this book. The stratigraphic analysis of 1037 resulted in the recognition of a group of related excavation loci, consisting of rooms or other activity areas, and these were numbered 1–12. They constituted the recoverable part of House 1037 (Fig. 12). Within each locus, identified walls, floors, and other building elements were arranged into a structural sequence, in relative chronological order wherever that was detectable (Fig. 13). Pottery contained in deposits within each locus, or associated with specific constructional elements, provided generalized absolute dating, to which five calibrated radiocarbon dates also contributed (OxCal 2012; OxCal 2016); (see notes on Table 1 for details of the chronology used below). The results of this analysis, arranged from

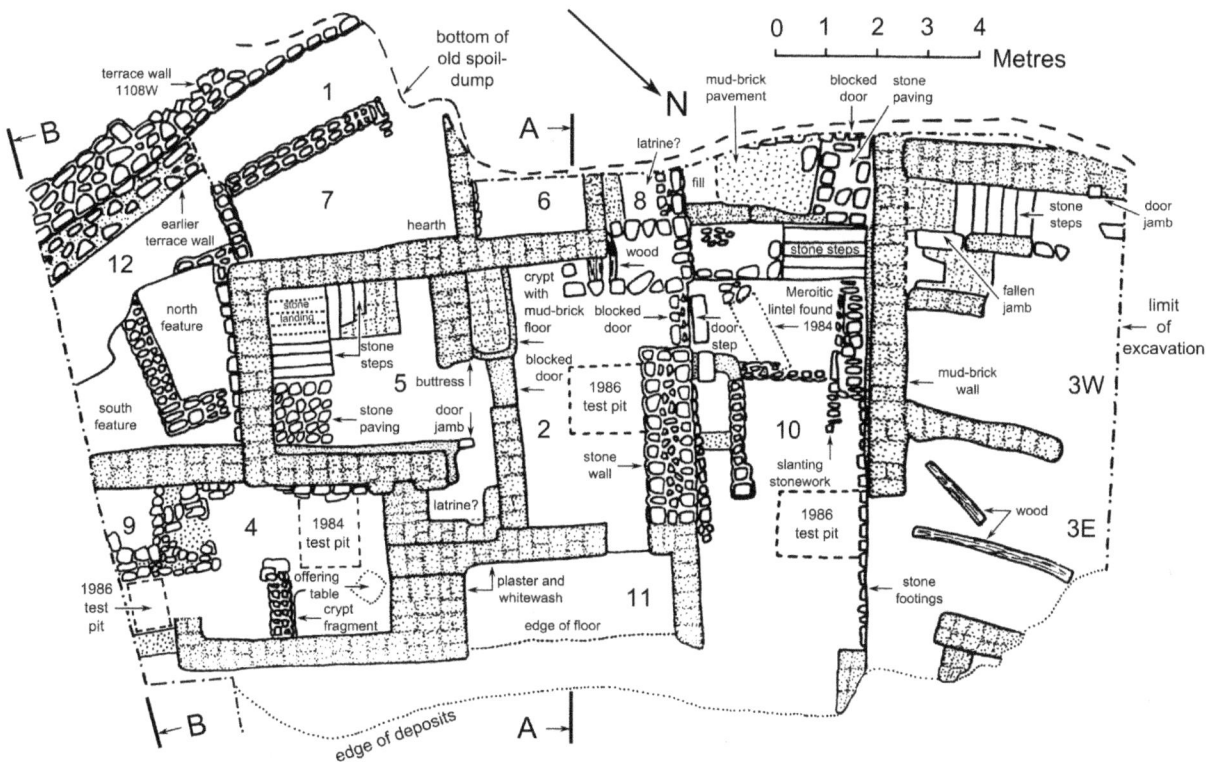

Fig. 12. Plan of House 1037 at the end of the 1986 excavation. Loci are numbered 1–12 for comparison with the structural sequence. 1 is a possible street, 2–11 are rooms, 12 is a midden outside the structure. Based on an unpublished draft by Lawrence Smith.

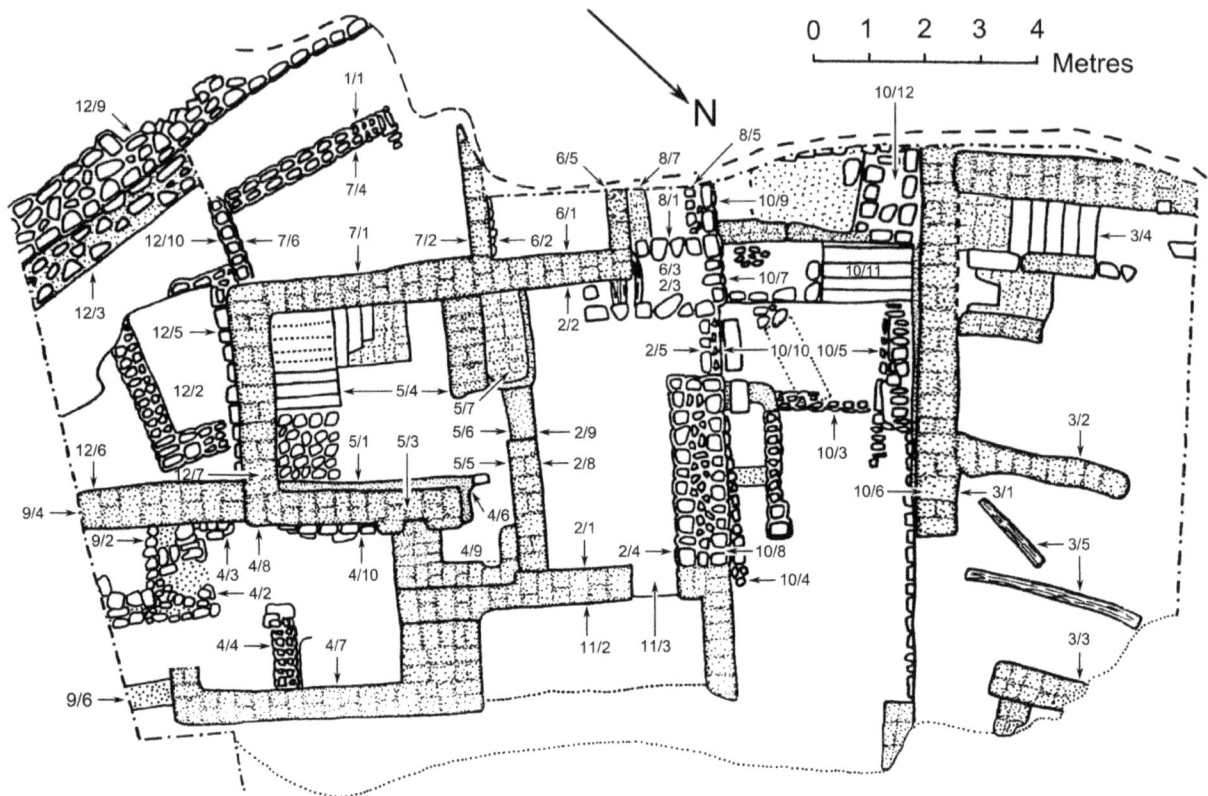

Fig. 13. Plan of House 1037 as in Fig. 12 but showing locus and phase numbers that are used in the structural sequence. Only structural features visible on the plan are numbered. Based on an unpublished draft by Lawrence Smith.

early to late for each locus, were as follows. (Locus and phase numbers are given, for example, as '1/3', the earliest being /1.) This list is most easily understood if examined in conjunction with the plans in Figures 12 and 13.

4

The Structural Sequence of House 1037

Note: structural features called 'crypts' in the following list are 'deep square or rectangular' underfloor storage spaces described by Adams and Adams (2013: 29) as 'a unique feature of many [Ballaña] houses'. Less formal storage pits are sometimes also so described. It is uncertain whether storage of valuables (Adams and Adams 2013: 41) or of grain (Adams and Adams 2013: 65) or other food was intended.

Locus 1: Street
(In the excavation field records this was called 'Street 1'.)

No pottery date.

1: Stone wall east side. Same as 7/4. Parallel with 12/9, forming street but 12/9 has traces of mud plaster from earlier structure.
2: Midden accumulated in street, burying stump of 1/1. Construction of 12/9, which cut through 12/8, also disturbed 1/2 but at a lower level. 1/2 similar to 7/5 and contemporary with 12/8.

Locus 2: Room

Pottery date* for locus *AD400–850: X-Group and Early Christian. Beta–44131 radiocarbon date for 0–40cm below Early Christian floor level: calibrated to: AD71–426 (Table 1).

1: Mud-brick wall to east. Same as 11/2 & 4/7 wall before (latrine?), earlier than 5/3 wall. Base of 2/1 below Early Christian floors (2/7), dated XC2 on pottery that is most probably intrusive. See calibrated radiocarbon date above.
2: Mud-brick wall to west. Same as 5/3 wall but misalignment probably suggests a later addition. Same as 6/1.
3: Mud-mortared stone structure with 2 timber reinforcements, stone rubble and earth. Later than 2/2. West side of structure same as 8/1, 6/3 & 10/7.
4: North wall of Locus 2, similar stonework and timber reinforcement to 2/3, probably same date; contains doorway to which probably belonged stone lintel with Meroitic text and

Fig. 14. Blocked doorway in wall between Locus 10 and Locus 2, from north-west, 30 January 1986. Scale in 10-cm divisions. Photograph by Tony Bonner.

symbols (the latter partly erased probably in Early Christian times) (See Fig. 47). Same as south wall of 10/8.

5: Doorway Loci 2–10 blocked, south side carefully finished, north side rough. Blocked before Early Christian floors (2/7) laid. Same as 10/10 (Fig. 14).

6: Midden.

7: Series of floors laid, Early Christian (on pottery). (Adams and Adams 2013: 44 record an example of three successive floors in a structure at Qasr Ibrim and another example of four successive floors, indicating 'fairly long period[s] of occupation'.)

8: Mud-brick and stone wall, with doorway, south of Locus 2. Same as 5/5.

9: Doorway from Loci 2–5, in 2/8 wall, blocked. Same as 5/6.

10: Midden.

Locus 3: Room (E & W)

Pottery date* for locus *AD400–600: X-Group.

1: Mud-brick east–west wall: south wall of 3E and 3W. Same as 10/6.

2: Mud-brick south–north wall, butted against 3/1 wall at acute angle forming west wall of Locus 3E and east wall of 3W. North face of 3/1 in 3E and east face of 3/2 in 3E mud-

Fig. 15. Steps in Locus 3W and Locus 10, also showing blocked doorway between Locus 10 and Locus 2. From north-west, 6 February 1986. Background scale in 10-cm divisions, foreground scale in 1-cm divisions. Photograph by Tony Bonner.

plastered and whitewashed so internal wall surfaces. (Compare with Adams and Adams 2013: 36 where: 'All the interior walls were smoothly plastered and whitewashed' in House X–221.)

3: Possible fragment of mud-brick east wall of Locus 3E at eastern limits of excavation.

4: Five stone steps between mud-brick walls, west side of Locus 3W (Fig. 15). Later than 3/1 but relationship to 3/2 & 3/3 unknown. Steps are in passageway with two stone door-jambs at north end and access to the rest of 3W to east. Relationship of 3W stone steps to 10/11 stone steps unclear, because 3/1 mud-brick wall here uncertain, but mud-brick pavement and fallen door-jamb at the top of 3W steps indicate access to west end of Locus 10, at a similar level. To east of 3W steps is a fragment of the south–north mud-brick wall attached to 3/1 wall, with more mud-brick attached to its eastern side.

5: Roof of Locus 3E collapsed: at least two roof beams left in debris filling room (Fig. 16).

6: Crypts in 3E and 3W, most to east, less in centre, few in west. Pottery XC1: AD550–600 (Figs 17 and 18).

7: Midden in crypts.

8. South–north stone wall of Islamic date at eastern side of site.

Fig. 16. Fallen roof timbers in Locus 3 from the north-east, 6 February 1986. Scale in 1-cm divisions. Photograph by Tony Bonner.

Fig. 17. Late storage pits in Locus 3, from the north-east, 30 January 1986. Scale in 10-cm divisions. Photograph by Tony Bonner.

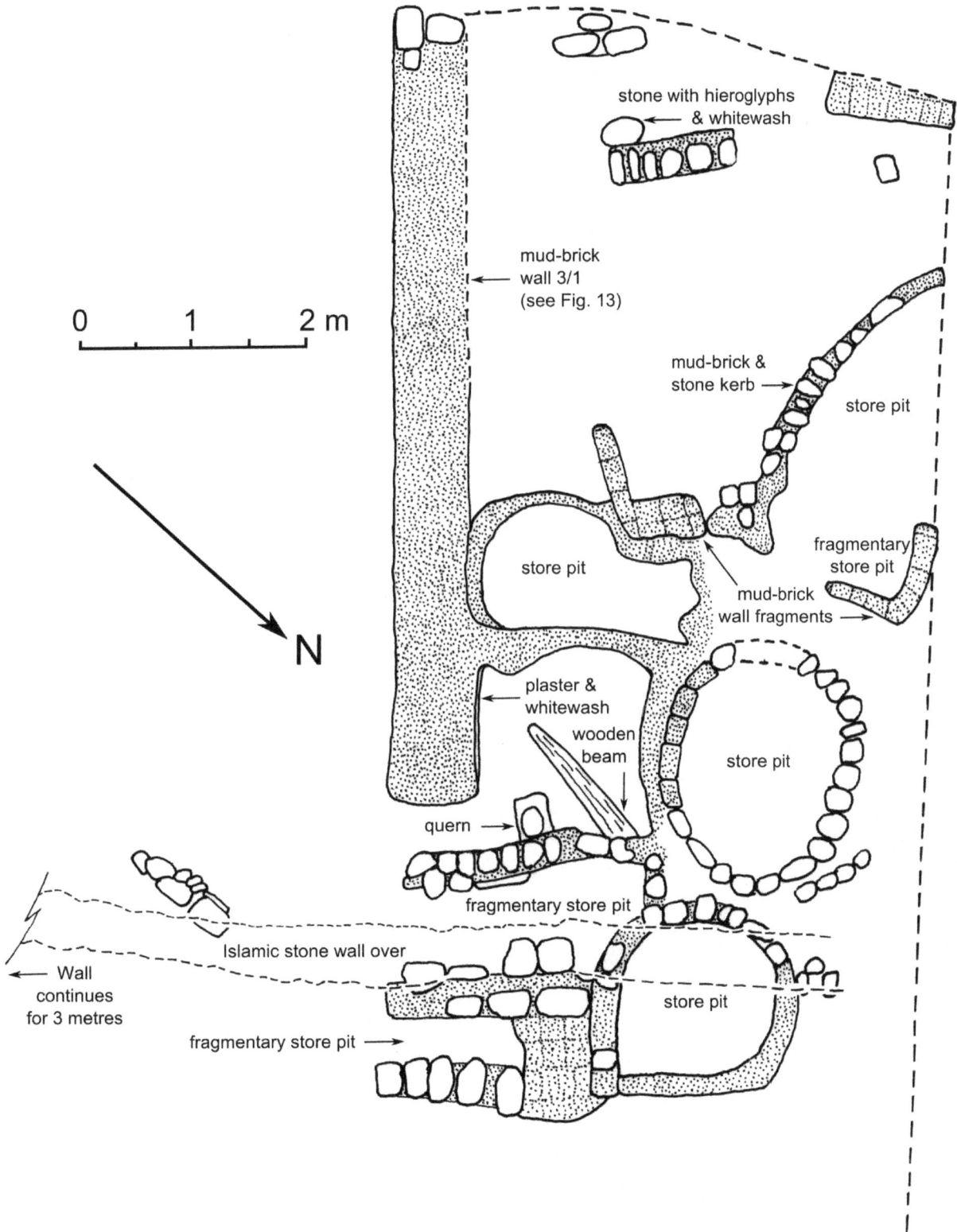

Fig. 18. Plan of late features in Locus 3. Compare with Fig. 17. These features overlay those of Locus 3 shown in Figs 12 and 13. After an unpublished draft by Lawrence Smith, redrawn by Graham Connah.

Locus 4: Room

Pottery date for locus *23 BC–AD550: mostly Meroitic and X-Group, residual Roman.*

1: Midden, not excavated to base. Contained Meroitic offering table (Fig. 19), (see Adams and Adams 2013: 210, where listed as a 'sandstone offering table' of the Ballaña Phase but without a Registration Number, although it does have a Day Number of 86.2.3/14 that matches the Artefact Index Card).

2: Stone-rubble L-shaped structure. Same as 9/2. Constructed during formation of 4/1. East–west stone wall above but not on excavation plan.

3: Fragment of stone wall, north–south from northern side of 9/2 and possibly contemporary with it.

4: Stone-built crypt east–west, in upper 4/1. Below 4/7 and therefore earlier. Wall of crypt partly slanting stonework, similar to 10/3 (Fig. 20).

5: Midden over 4/1–4/4.

6: Lower mud-brick west wall Locus 4. Same as 12/6, 5/1 and 9/4. Locus 4 had series of pink cement floors and mud floors.

7: Mud-brick north and east walls of Locus 4. Predate 4/8. Perhaps contemporary with 4/6. Same as 2/1 and 11/2.

Fig. 19. Two pieces of a Meroitic sandstone offering-table (86.2.3/14) in the side of a 1984 test-pit, Locus 4. View from north-east, 30 January 1986. Scale in 1-cm divisions. Photograph by Tony Bonner.

Fig. 20. Locus 4 from the south-east, showing partly slanting stonework probably of X-Group date, 6 February 1986. Scale in 10-cm divisions. Compare with Adams and Adams (2013: 237, Plate 4c). Photograph by Tony Bonner.

8: Upper mud-brick west wall Locus 4 constructed on top of 4/6 wall, but out-of-line. East-facing surface of 4/8 wall mud-plastered and whitewashed. Same as 5/3, 12/7 and 7/1.

9: Small mud-brick room constructed in north-west corner Locus 4. Its mud-brickwork over whitewashed mud plaster of 4/8 and therefore later. Latrine? Entered by doorway from Locus 5.

10: Stone wall, mud-mortared. Against east face of 4/8, probably as support because of lean to east of 4/8 (Fig. 21).

11: Midden filled Locus 4.

Locus 5: Room

Pottery date for locus *AD400–850: X-Group and Early Christian.*

1: Lower east mud-brick wall. Same as 4/6, 12/6 and 9/4.

2: Midden filled area west of 5/1.

3: Upper east, south and west mud-brick walls. Same as 4/8, 12/7, 7/1 and possibly earlier than 2/2 but later than 2/1. Probable winnowing floor and mud-brick floor above assumed contemporary with walls.

Fig. 21. Stone wall from the north-east, probably intended to support a mud-brick wall leaning to the north-east, 30 January 1986. Locus 4 in foreground, Locus 5 in background. Scale in 10-cm divisions. Photograph by Tony Bonner.

4: Three very worn stone steps, leading to landing of four stone slabs and mud-brick support for three steps. Stone paving at base of steps. Mud-brick buttress for possible upper timber stair to north of steps (Fig. 22). (Adams and Adams 2010 and 2013 mention several structures at Qasr Ibrim where the presence of a staircase could imply the existence of an upper storey.)

5: Mud-brick and stone wall, with doorway, same as 2/8, to north of Locus 5 and over 2/7 floors with Early Christian pottery dates. 5/5 butts against east wall of Locus 2 and (latrine?) wall of Locus 4 and therefore later than 4/9.

6: Doorway from Loci 2–5, in 5/5 wall, blocked. Same as 2/9.

7: Mud-brick-floored crypt through south wall of Locus 2 and to north of 5/4 buttress.

8: Midden filled Locus 5.

Locus 6: Room

Pottery date** for locus **AD350–550: Meroitic and X-Group.

1: Mud-brick wall to east. Same as 2/2.

2: Mud-brick wall to south on top of stone wall. Both butted against 6/1 wall, therefore later. Same as 7/2.

Fig. 22. Stone steps in Locus 5, from the east, about 30 December 1985. Scale in 1-cm divisions. Photograph by Tony Bonner.

3: Mud-mortared stone structure with two timber reinforcements, same as 2/3, 10/7 and 8/1. Later than 6/1 but unknown chronological relationship to 6/2.

4: Midden and stone and mud-brick rubble fill. Much pottery, including intact pots, AD350–550. Probably crypt.

5: Mud-brick wall to north, on top of 6/4, which continues as 6/6. Wall parallel to 8/7.

6: Midden etc, as 6/4, continues.

Locus 7: Room

Pottery date for locus AD350–500: Meroitic and X-Group.

1: Mud-brick wall to east, forming west wall of Locus 5. Same as 12/7, 5/3 and 4/8.

2: Mud-brick wall built to north, butted against 5/3 and therefore later. Same as 6/2.

3: Mud floor with traces of cement over. Fireplace north-east corner. (Adams and Adams 2013: 41 comment on 'the conspicuous rarity of fireplaces' in the earlier Ballaña period at Qasr Ibrim.)

4: Stone wall to west, same as 1/1. Fragment of stone wall butts on northern end. Relationship to 7/3 unknown.

5: South part of 7/3 floor destroyed, replaced by midden similar to 1/2.

6: Stone wall south side of Locus 7. Same as 12/10, butts against 7/4 and 5/3, lies over 7/5.

Locus 8: Room

Pottery date **for locus** *AD350–650: Meroitic and X-Group.*

1: Mud-mortared stone structure with two timber reinforcements, to east. Same as 2/3, 10/7 and 6/3.

2: Midden. Similar to 6/4. Pottery AD350–400.

3: Mud-brick floor over part of 8/2, under 8/7.

4: Midden. Similar to 6/4 but date unknown.

5: Stone wall to north, upper part mud-brick. Butted against west face of 8/1. Same as 10/9.

6: Midden. Similar to 6/4 but date unknown.

7: Mud-brick wall to south over timber resting on top of 8/1 and over 8/3 floor. Wall parallel to 6/5.

8: Midden.

Locus 9: Room

Pottery date **for locus** *c.720 BC–AD350: mostly Meroitic, residual Napatan and Roman.*

1: Midden with fragments of bedrock, over bedrock sloping to east.

2: Stone-rubble L-shaped structure, over 9/1. Same as 4/2. East–west stone wall above on photographs of excavation at an early stage.

3: Midden over 9/2.

4: Mud-brick wall to west over 9/3. Same as 12/6, 4/6 and 5/1.

5: Horizontally-banded deposits from face of 9/4 to east and above 9/3. Possibly mud floors.

6: Mud-brick wall to east. Built while 9/5 forming, butted against fragment of south wall of 4/7, so later.

7: Midden buried remains of Locus 9.

8: Modern lake deposits and spoil-dump.

Locus 10: Room

Pottery date **for locus** *c.720 BC–AD550: mostly X-Group (AD400–550).* **Napatan, Roman** **and X-Group in test-pit.** Beta–44133 radiocarbon date for 120–160cm below top of north wall: calibrated to: 352BC–AD132 (Table 1).

1: Midden over bedrock surface, to maximum depth of 2.95 metres.

2: Mass of mud-brick-work in top 90–95cm of 1986 test-pit, unidentified structure. Associated pottery suggests Napatan, Roman or X-Group date. The test-pit was 2.0–2.95m deep, with its bottom on bedrock; the lower part contained Napatan pottery and gave a radiocarbon date (Beta–72854) calibrated to: 1218–895BC (Table 1).

3: Parts of north, south and west walls of stone structure, north and south wall partly slanting stonework similar to 4/4. (Żurawski (2013: 124) mentions Roman and Kushite use of vertical and slanting masonry, called in Latin *opus spicatum*, which he calls 'a hallmark of the earliest medieval fortifications in the [Nubian] region'. For other photographs of vertical masonry see Eigner (2013: 314). Similar stonework at Qasr Ibrim, called 'herringbone' construction, is illustrated in Adams and Adams (2013: 237, Plate 4c), where it is described as 'found in some late Ballaña walls'.) South wall roughly parallel to later stone walls 10/4 and 10/7. Mud-brickwork joins south wall of 10/3 to later stone walls in two places.

4: Stone wall running east–west beneath 10/8 but chronological relationship to other phases unknown.

5: Stone wall running east–west, over stump of north wall of 10/3, originally probably extended to east. Its west end butted against mud-brick wall 10/11 but is presumed earlier; its north face under mud-brick wall 10/6.

6: Mud-brick wall to north. Sits on stone footings of 10/5. Same as 3/1.

7: Mud-mortared stone structure with two timber reinforcements. Same as 2/3, 6/3 and 8/1.

8: Stone wall running east–west between Loci 10 and 2. Same as 2/4. Status doorway between 10/7 and 10/8, with door-jambs, steps, and a lintel inscribed in Meroitic (see Fig. 47). Doorway probably open in Meroitic, X-Group and Early Christian periods and lintel symbols defaced in latter. Lintel found 1984 displaced in fill of Locus 10, indicating probable location over doorway. Length of lintel was 163cm, space between outside edges of the finely cut sandstone jambs was 133cm, so the ends of the lintel must have rested on the wall masonry beyond the outside edges of the jambs, if the lintel was from above this doorway (Connah 1986c: 129).

9: Stone wall running east–west, forming north wall of Locus 8. Butted against west face of 2/3. Same as 8/5.

10: Doorway between Loci 2 and 10 blocked (Figs 14 and 15), south side blocking carefully finished, north side rough. Blocked before Early Christian floors 2/7. Chronological relationship to later phases unknown. Same as 2/5.

11: Mud-brick wall constructed to west of Locus 10. Butted against south face of 10/6, supporting south–north stone wall and five stone steps. Also butted against north face of 10/7. Top step has X-Group pottery above: AD400–500 (Fig. 23).

12: Construction at top of stone steps, consisting of mud-brick south–north wall on stone footings and probably later than the south–north stone wall of 10/11. Stone-paved landing

Table 1: Analysis of House 1037 pottery evidence (on-site identifications by Pamela Rose)

Locus	Level	Location	Pottery date	C14 years BP (wood)	Calibrated
2 (room)	0–40cm	Below EC floor level	XC2	Beta–44131: 1770+/–80	AD71–426
2 (room)	0–40cm	Test-pit	XC1		
2 (room)	40–80cm	Test-pit	LSC–MX/X1?		
2 (room W)	0–30cm		EC2		
2 (room W)	30–60cm		EC2		
2 (room W)	60–90cm	With group of pots	EC2		
2 (room W)	90–120cm		EC2		
3 (room)	0–40cm	Area of room	Contaminated–Mixed, bulk X		
3 (room E)		Defining structures	X1		
3 (room E)		Fill of crypts	XC1		
3 (room E)		Removal of crypts	XC1		
3 (room W)	Area	Defining structures	LSC		
3 (room W)	40–80cm		XC1		
4 (room)		S wall & fill beneath	Contaminated–RM		
4 (room)	Level 1	Lower fill	MX		
4 (room)	Pit 1	Fill	X1		
4 (room)	50–75cm	SW corner, defining mud wall	LSC–Latest X		
4 (room S)	50–80cm	Below top of W wall	MX/X1		
4 (room SW)		Rubble & fill	Mixed, bulk M		
4/9 (room)		Doorway & common wall	M1?		
4/9 (room)		Doorway blocking	LSC		
4/9 (room)		Fill over rubble spill	RM?		
5 (room NW)	0–20cm		Mix, bulk XC2–10% later sherds		
5 (room NW)	20/40–40/60cm		EC1		
5 (room NW)	60–80cm		XC1		
5 (room NW)	80–110cm	And central W	EC2		
5 (room)	0–40cm	Area S	X1		
6 (room E)	0–30cm		X2		
6 (room E)	30–60cm		X1/X2		
6 (room E)	60–90cm		X1/X2		
6 (room E)	90–120cm		MX/X1		
7 (room E)	0–40cm		MX/X1		
8? (room)	0–30cm	Fill	Mixed: X—XC		
8 (room W)	Fill to 30cm	Below top of stonework	MX		
9 (room)		Fill at W end	RM		
9 (room)		Basal rubble and fill, N side	N—RM		
9 (room N)	0–40cm		M		
10 (room)	120–160cm	Below top N wall	X1	Beta–44133: 2030+/–80	352BC–AD132
10 (room)	0–40cm	Below top N wall, room fill	X1		
10 (room)	40–80cm	Below top N wall, room fill	X1 and later contamination		

Locus	Level	Location	Pottery date	C14 years BP (wood)	Calibrated
10 (room)	80–120cm	Below top N wall, room fill	X1 and later contamination		
10 (room W)	40–80cm		X1		
10 (room W)		On level top step	X1		
10 (room)	0–75cm	Test-pit	Mixed: N–Bulk X1; X2		
10 (room)	75cm–2m	Test-pit	Mixed: N–Bulk R; X		
10 (room)	2m–bedrock	Test-pit	N1	Beta–72854: 2860+/– 60	1218–895BC
11 (room W)		Upper fill and unstratified	Bulk X1, trace LC/I		
12 (area)	Level 1	Carbonized material & soil	M2	Beta–44132: 1720+/–70	AD130–531
12 (area)	Level 2	Foundation trench fill, terrace wall	R2		
12 (area)	Level 3	Lower carbonized soil	M2		
12 (area)	Level 4	Fill of S feature	R2		
12 (area)	Level 5	Fill of N feature	M1		
12 (area)	Level 5	Fill of N feature, W part	M1	Beta–72855: 1900+/– 80	89BC–AD330
12 (area)	Level 6	Fill of N feature, E part	M1		
12 (area)	Level 7	Mudbrick wall & fill E of S feature	R2		
12 (area)	0–40cm	Area	MX		
12 (area)	Below 40cm	Cleaning surface	MX		

Notes:

N1: Relative dating only but start corresponds approximately to the beginning of the 25th Dynasty, circa 720BC.

N2: Relative dating only.

N3: Relative dating only.

N4: Relative dating only.

P: (Ptolemaic) 100–23BC.

R1: 23BC–

R2: –AD100.

M1: AD100–200.

M2: AD200–350.

MX: AD350–400.

X1: AD400–500.

X2: AD500–550.

XC1: AD550–600.

XC2: AD600–650.

EC1: AD650–750.

EC2: AD750–850.

CC1: AD850–1000.

CC2: AD1000–1100.

LC1: AD1100–1300.

LC2: AD1300–1400.

TC: AD1400–1500.

I: AD1500–

Dates separated by / indicate that the material could belong to either group.

'Mixed' usually applies to pit fills.

The use of a letter code without a supplementary phase number means that the date cannot be more precise.

LSC = Low sherd count; less than 70 sherds.

Fig. 23. Locus 10 from the north-east, showing steps in the background and a test-pit in right foreground, 30 January 1986. The test-pit was 2.0–2.95m deep, with its bottom on bedrock; it gave a radiocarbon date (on wood) of cal 1218–895BC (Table 1). Scale in 10-cm divisions. Photograph by Tony Bonner.

at top of steps, in front of doorway (which was later blocked) in south–north stone wall at extreme west of excavation. Landing led to mud-brick-paved area to south between south–north mud-brick wall and south–north stone wall at extreme west.

13: Midden, continued an intermittent accumulation.

Locus 11: Room

***Pottery date** for locus mostly X-Group (AD400–500), traces of Late Christian (1100–1300).*

1: Midden.

2: Mud-brick wall to west. Its east face whitewashed mud plaster, continuing onto northern face of south wall. Same as 2/1 and 4/7 before insertion of 4/9.

3: Doorway between Loci 11 and 2 at pre-Early-Christian floor level. North side of doorway and north mud-brick wall of Locus 11 added to north stone wall 2/4. Uncertain whether doorway and north mud-brick wall contemporary with 11/2.

4: Midden.

Locus 12: Open space

Pottery date **for locus** *mostly Meroitic (AD100–400), some Roman.*

In excavation field records this was called 'Area South of Room 5'. Beta–44132 radiocarbon date for Level 1, carbonized material and soil: calibrated to: AD130—531 (Table 1).

1: Thin midden over bedrock.

2: Crypt into bedrock and into 12/1. Stone walls upper south, east, and north sides (Fig. 24). Beta–72855 radiocarbon date for Level 5, fill of north feature, west part: calibrated to: 89BC–AD330 (Table 1).

3: Stone revetment wall against a drop in bedrock west of 12/2; locus an open space. Relationship to 12/2 and 12/4 unknown.

4: Midden accumulated in crypt 12/2.

5: Stone wall across crypt 12/2, east–west, after crypt partly filled with 12/4. Wall below 12/7. Blocked-up doorway in stonework (Fig. 25).

6: Mud-brick wall to east of crypt 12/2. Same as 5/1, 9/4 and 4/6.

Fig. 24. Locus 12 from the south, showing (to left and right) so-called 'north' and 'south' features (Fig. 12) and earlier stonework overlain by later mud-brick walls, 9 February 1986. The western part of the fill of the north feature gave a radiocarbon date (on wood) of cal 89BC–AD330 (Table 1). Scale in 10-cm divisions. Photograph by Tony Bonner.

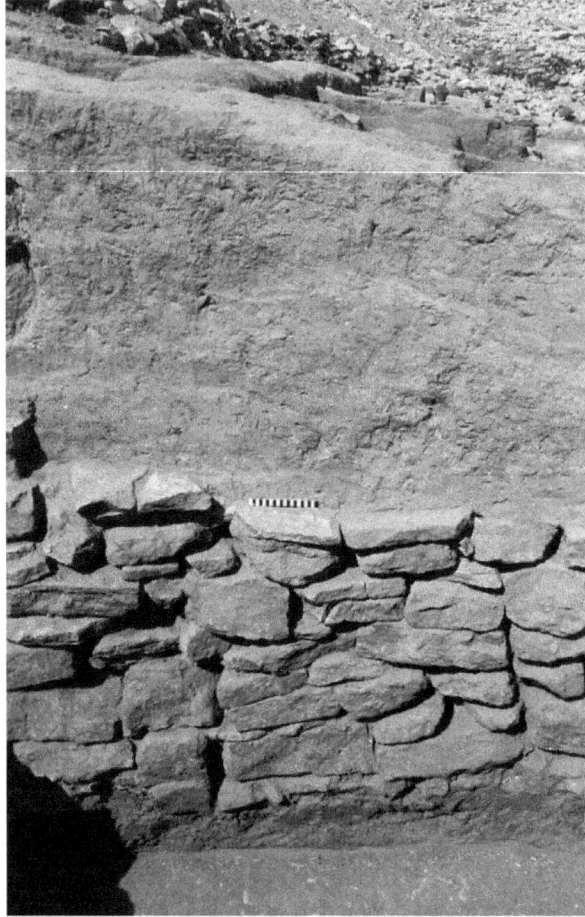

Fig. 25. South-east mud-brick wall of Locus 5, from Locus 12 to its south-east, showing blocked-up doorway in earlier stonework. Scale in 1-cm divisions. Photograph by Graham Connah.

7: Mud-brick wall 12/7 over 12/5 and 12/6. Same as 5/3, 4/8 and 7/1 (Fig. 26).

8: Midden above crypt 12/2: horizontal deposits bounded by 12/3, 12/6, and 5/7. Same as 1/2.

9: Stone revetment wall replaced 12/3 revetment wall, which was robbed almost to its footings, cutting through some deposits of 12/8 (Fig. 27).

10: Stone wall south side of Locus 7. Same as 7/6. Later than 12/8 but relationship to 12/9 unknown.

Fig. 26. Site 1037 from the south-east, 23 January 1986. Locus 12 in the foreground was only partly excavated at this time; mud-brick wall 12/7 is in foreground and Locus 5 behind it. Scale in 10-cm divisions. Photograph by Tony Bonner.

Fig. 27. Locus 12, showing later revetment wall 12/9 overlying earlier revetment wall 12/3, 23 January 1986. From the east. Photograph by Tony Bonner.

5

Interpreting the Structural Sequence of House 1037

The above structural sequence resulted from a detailed analysis of the 1986 excavation records during 2012–2014. It is apparent that the stratification of the site was complex and that its stratigraphic taphonomy needed close attention. The house site appeared to have been continuously occupied, or at least there was no recognizable evidence of a break in that occupation. Evidence for continuity consisted of repeated accumulation of stratigraphic units, without intervening sterile deposits. There was also the construction of walls, floors and other features at different times, some over the top of or against older ones. In addition, doorways were blocked up (compare for example Adams and Adams 2010: 15, 19, 61 Plate 3d; 2013: 33, 36, 42, 43). Renovations and replacements were carried out, wall plaster and floors covered older structural elements, different construction methods were utilized, crypts or storage pits were dug, and a set of stone steps in Locus 5, leading to an upper floor or upper level on the sloping site, had become very worn with use. In many cases there were only vestigial indications of the activities involved. It is nevertheless possible that parts of the structural complex were disused at times, as indicated by the accumulation of midden material in some rooms. Furthermore, as the associated pottery and calibrated radiocarbon dates show, all this happened over at least seven centuries, not counting residual evidence from earlier periods and superimposed later evidence that had been removed by erosion during high lake levels or by excavation in 1984. This is a house onto which it is difficult to put neat cultural or chronological labels.

On Site 1037 construction was in both stone and mud-brick. As Adams and Adams (2013: 29) commented:

> The Qasr Ibrim citadel was nearly unique among Nubian sites in that, from Ballaña times onward, the great majority of domestic architecture was in stone rather than mud brick. This was perhaps sufficiently explained by the elevated situation, where mud bricks had to be carried up from the riverbank far below, while stone could be quarried anywhere on the nearby mountaintop. Mud brick, in Ballaña times, was used mainly for interior partitions; particularly those inserted subsequent to the original building of the houses.

The use mud-brick as well as stone at Site 1037 would suggest that the former material was nevertheless preferred at times, despite its laborious transport from the riverbank. Carrying stones could also have required substantial effort and, because of their irregular shape and size, building with them could have been more time-consuming than building in mud-bricks that were each of a similar size and shape.

A plan of the site at the end of the excavation in 1986 shows the complexity of the structural evidence (Fig. 12). This should be compared with the same plan on which are marked the locus and phase numbers used in the 1986 structural sequence (Fig. 13). Although presenting only a relative sequence with limited absolute control, these plans provide more information than the generalized structural plans that often characterized excavation at Qasr Ibrim before 1986 (Fig. 3). Also, the 1986 plans present horizontal data that can be considered in the context of the vertical data. Most of the excavated features had little surviving deposit over them, as shown in a section (Fig. 28) along the line A–A on Figure 12. In contrast, a section along the line B–B, on the same figure, was through a deep midden deposit outside the building complex (Fig. 29). Consequently, Site 1037 conformed to the general stratification at Qasr Ibrim, comprising standing remains of buildings, fallen or displaced remains of buildings, and midden deposits within and around buildings (W.Y. Adams 1996: 8). At 1037 the first two types of stratification provided most of the structural evidence but comparatively few associated artefacts except potsherds; the third type had little structural evidence but numerous and diverse artefacts, including organic items preserved in spite of submergence by the lake for several years before 1986. In addition, the site had been occupied before the construction of the building complex that was investigated in 1986. The lowest deposits at the site were sampled with four test-pits, one excavated by Alexander in 1984 and three by GC in 1986. According to Alexanders's unpublished field records (archived at the British Museum), at Site 1037 there were: 'Three separate phases represented. Probably Islamic, Christian and

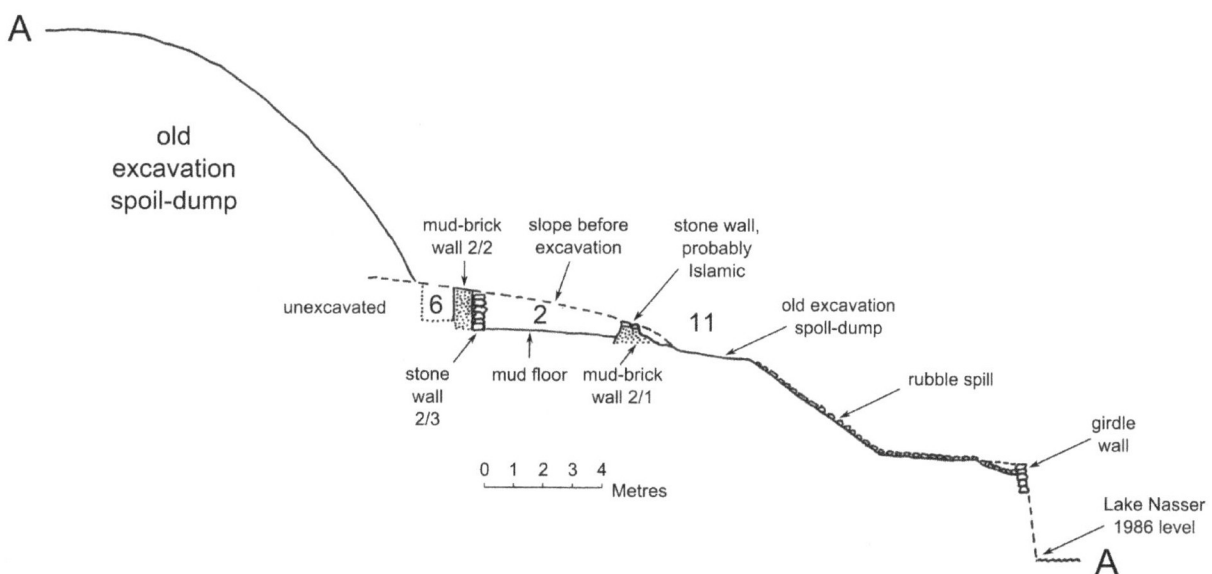

Fig. 28. North-west section A–A on Fig. 12, showing the shallow surviving deposits over the structural remains. Scale is approximate. Based on an unpublished draft by Lawrence Smith, redrawn by Graham Connah.

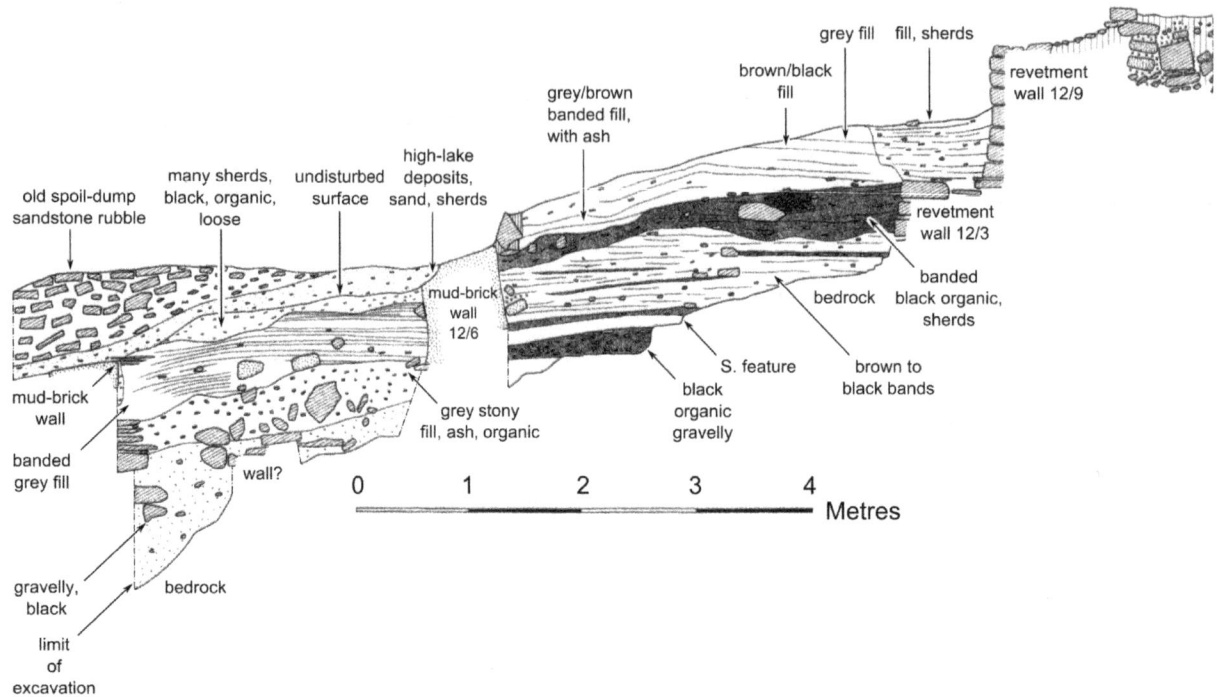

Fig. 29. South-east section B–B on Fig. 12, showing organic-rich midden deposits. Stones are hatched, mud-brick is stippled. Based on a field-drawing by Graham Connah and Chris Caley, redrawn by Douglas Hobbs.

X-Group. Bedrock not reached anywhere' (Alexander 1984b: 59). Significantly, the earlier deposits revealed in 1986 were not investigated in 1984. Of the 1986 test-pits, bedrock was reached at 1.82 metres below the level of 9/6 in Room 9, at 2.95 metres below the general excavation level in Room 10, and was not reached at 0.80 metres below a similar level in Room 2 (Fig. 12). Parts of an unidentified mud-brick structure were located at a depth between 0.90 and 0.95 metres below the general excavation level in the Room 10 test-pit. These earlier deposits were not relevant to the research objective of the 1986 excavation, and they were not investigated further. Nevertheless, residual pottery that was recovered included Napatan material dating from about 720 BC, as well as Roman material of the first century AD. It should also be noticed that, in Locus 12, midden deposits excavated to bedrock contained some of the earliest reliably dated pottery from the site, including Roman as well as Meroitic (Fig. 30).

No obvious structures of either Napatan or Roman date were found on Site 1037, suggesting the presence of residual material in garbage from occupation higher up the slope to the west, or indicating that excavation was too limited to reveal such structures. However, Roman pottery was found in a pit immediately to the west of the terrace wall 1108W, and also higher up the slope where shallow deposits of little more than 30 centimetres over the bedrock surface, and shallow pits cut into the bedrock, produced pottery of Napatan, Roman, possibly Meroitic, Late Christian, and Islamic date, together with fragmentary structural remains. The vestigial and mixed character of this evidence from west of 1037 and from nearby (so-called) 'Stable

	1	2	3	4	5	6	7	8	9	10	11	12
I											Trace	
TC											Trace	
LC2											Trace	
LC1											Trace	
CC2												
CC1												
EC2		Known			Known							
EC1					Known							
XC2		Known	Mixed		Known			Mixed				
XC1		Known	Known		Known							
X2		Mixed				Known				Known		
X1		Mixed	Known	Known	Known	Known		Known		Known	Known	
MX		Mixed		Known	Known	Known	Known	Known	Mixed			Known
M2				Mixed					Mixed			Known
M1				Mixed					Mixed			Known
R2				Mixed					Residual	Mixed		Known
R1				Mixed					Residual	Mixed		
P									Residual	Mixed		
N4									Residual	Mixed		
N3									Residual	Mixed		
N2									Residual	Mixed		
N1									Residual	Known		

Known Dates	(orange)
Mixed Dates	(blue)
Residual Dates	(yellow)
Trace	(gray)

Fig. 30. Chronological reliability of the pottery from Site 1037, suggesting a date range of mainly Meroitic to Early Christian but with some Napatan and Roman material. Note: there is no pottery date for Locus 1. Compiled by David Pearson but see Mattingly 2013: 390–96, where similar diagrams are used.

Street' limit its value and, as indicated previously, it is not considered in detail in this book (see Page 5).

Because the chronology of the structures excavated in 1986 is so dependent on pottery dates, it is important to consider the provenances and general contexts of the pottery. First, with some exceptions, the excavated pots and sherds relate to the fill of rooms not to the construction of the walls, floors or other features of the rooms. Second, for Locus 12 they are relevant to the period during which a midden accumulated. These circumstances indicate that the pottery was probably mostly later in date than the structures themselves, although in some cases possibly earlier given the presence of residual sherds at the site. Third, the dates presented in this book are those that were determined by Pamela Rose, the pottery analyst on the site at the time of the 1986 excavation. These determinations were based on the typology used by W.Y. Adams (1986) in his study of medieval Nubian pottery and, given the present state of knowledge, might now need revision. However, the material itself is no longer available and cannot be re-examined. The pottery analysis indicates the problems of interpretation that have resulted from these circumstances (Table 1). Pottery that can be reliably dated and is relevant to the structural sequence is shown in red on Fig. 30 (i.e. excluding residual, test-pit, and second-millennium AD material). It ranges in date from Roman to Meroitic, to 'X-Group', to Early Christian. Nevertheless, the reliably dated pottery from Locus 12 was mainly Roman and Meroitic and came principally from midden deposits. Excluding this midden material leaves a main date-range for the structural sequence at the site of AD350–400, through to AD750–850. In addition, an analysis of all the pottery using a Harris Matrix shows a similar chronology and relates it to the loci and phases of the structural sequence (Fig. 31). The data remains difficult to interpret but it appears that the house represented by the structural sequence was characterized by residential continuity, in spite of cultural changes previously recognized at Qasr Ibrim.

Table 1 lists the pottery dates for the excavated loci at Site 1037 and a detailed key to the 22 phase designations in use is given in the notes at the base of that table. In their study of the Ballaña Phase of Qasr Ibrim, Adams and Adams (2013: 11) shorten this list to only 8, as follows:

M   Meroitic

X   Full Ballaña period

X1   Early Ballaña period

X2   Later Ballaña period

XC   Transitional period

EC   Early Christian period

CC   Classic Christian period

LC   Late Christian period

These generously bracket the occupation of the 1037 house but Adams and Adams (2013: 11) have warned that:

> For all the periods before the Classic Christian, these successive stages of occupation cannot be strictly differentiated on the basis of architectural stratigraphy alone. Most buildings remained in use for a period of several centuries, and their occupation extended over more than one phase … Phase designations are therefore based entirely on potsherd counts, according to the method in [*Ceramic industries of medieval Nubia*, Parts I and II (W.Y. Adams 1986)].

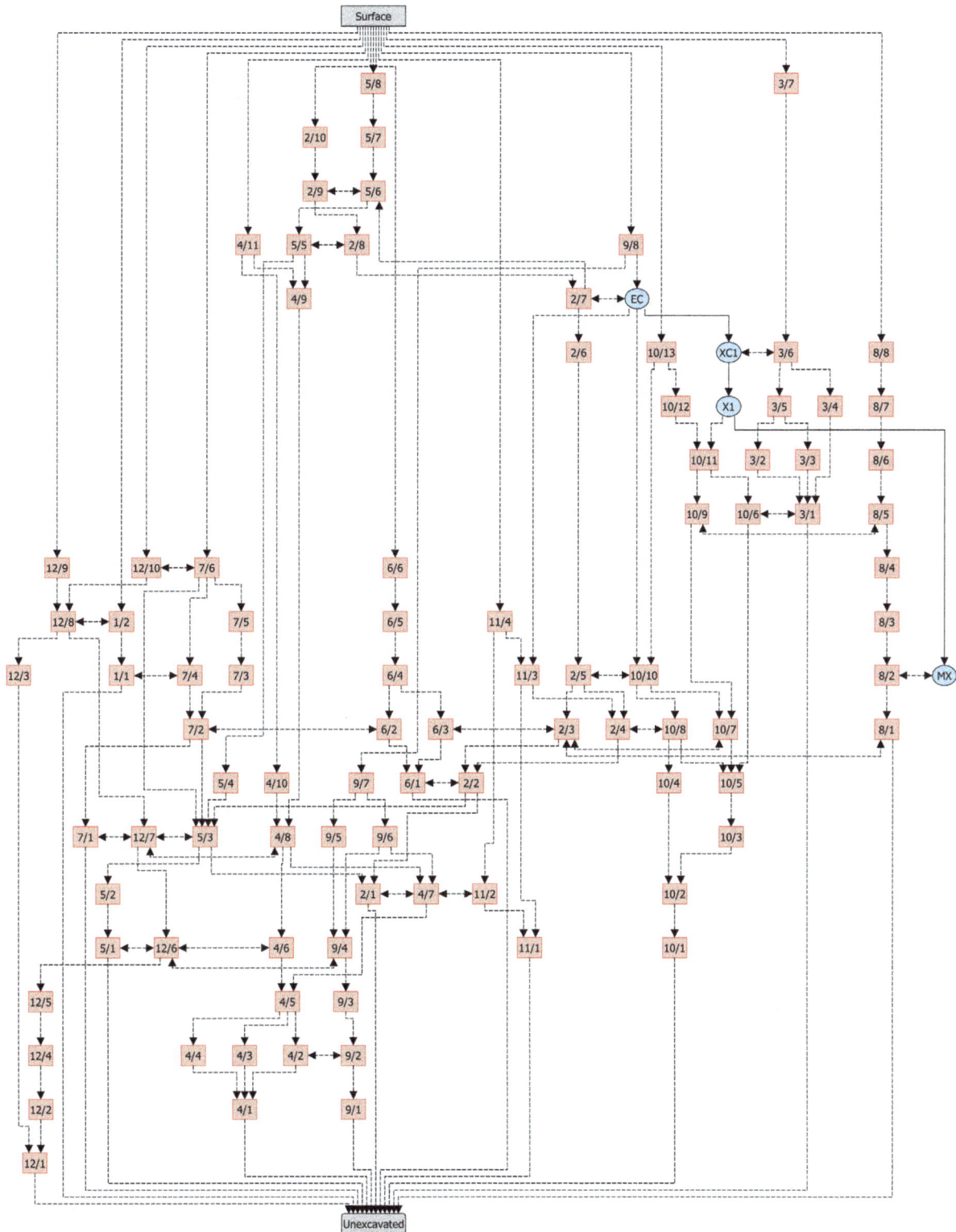

Fig. 31. Harris Matrix of the structural sequence at Site 1037, incorporating pottery dating where known. This suggests that loci (mostly rooms) were used over a considerable time, some through multiple cultural phases. The red boxes represent the structural sequence (compare phase numbers with Fig. 13). The blue ellipses represent a datable sequence based on the pottery chronology. Meroitic and pre-Meroitic loci/phases appear in the lower part of the matrix, X-Group loci/phases in the centre right and Early Christian or later in the upper left. Compiled by David Pearson.

They go on to explain that phase designations can also be used for domestic refuse deposits and the artefacts within them, noting that X1, X2 and XC indicate transitional phases in which X-Group sherds are mixed first with Meroitic sherds that are gradually replaced by Early Christian sherds. This they remark is a relative chronology, not an absolute one, and 'actual dating ... in nearly all cases is impossible'.

Implicit in the latter remark, there seems to have been little application of radiocarbon dating at Qasr Ibrim, so far as structural sequences are concerned, although Horton (1991) made some use of it in this manner and Rowley-Conwy (e.g. 1988; 1989) demonstrated its importance in faunal and botanical investigations. The reason for its near-neglect appears to have been because ceramic analysis 'will usually permit the dating of deposits within an interval of 100 years, and often of 50 years or even less' (W.Y. Adams 1996: 20). Indeed, for the Late Medieval Period, subsequent to the periods covered by this book, written texts excavated from the site can also provide dates. Nevertheless, five radiocarbon dates were obtained for Site 1037. Beta Analytic Inc., University Branch, Coral Gables, Florida, provided three of these in May 1991. Two others were received from Beta Analytic Inc., University Branch, Miami, Florida, in June 1994. The details for the 1991 dates (also given in Table 1) are as follows: Beta–44131: 1037 Locus 2, 0–40cm below Early Christian floor: 1770+/–80BP, wood. Beta–44132: 1037 Locus 12, Level 1, carbonized material and soil: 1720+/–70BP, wood. Beta 44133: 1037, Locus 10, 120–160cm below top of north wall: 2030+/–80, wood. These were calibrated (OxCal 2012) respectively to Beta–44131: AD71–426; Beta 44132: AD130–531; and Beta 44133: 352BC–AD132. The details for the 1994 dates (also given in Table 1) are as follows: Beta–72854: 1037 Locus 10. From lower part of test-pit from 2.0m to bedrock (bedrock sloped from 2.75 to 2.95m below lowest level of excavation in Locus 10: 160cm below top of north wall): 2860+/–60BP, wood. Beta–72855: 1037 Locus 12, Level 5, fill of north feature (western part), black, organic-rich, slightly gravelly deposit: 1900+/–80BP, wood. These were calibrated (OxCal 2016) respectively to: Beta–72854: 1218–895BC; Beta 72855: 89BC–AD330.

It is useful to compare these results with the pottery dates for the contexts of the samples submitted. Twigs of wood would have been preferred for the radiocarbon samples in each case, rather than pieces of mature timber that might give older dates than the deposits in which they were found, but the samples were mixed in this respect. As Adams (1996: 11) commented of Qasr Ibrim: '...wood was obviously scarce and valuable, so that large items of wood were routinely refashioned into smaller ones and perhaps ultimately were burned as fuel, after they had served their original purposes'. Beta–44131 indicates a date of AD71–426 compared with a pottery date of AD600–650 (Table 1), and comes from a locus that also contained pottery that was most probably intrusive, that is to say of later date. Therefore the radiocarbon date and the pottery date might not conflict with one another as much as it appears. Beta–44132 indicates a date of AD130–531 compared with a pottery date of AD200–350 (Table 1), and comes from a locus that also has some Roman pottery about a century older. In this case the two sources give dates that are closer. It is Beta–44133 that appears most problematic. It indicates a date of 352BC–AD132 compared with a pottery date of AD400–500 (Table 1). However, this radiocarbon sample was from a depth of 120–160cm and Napatan, Roman and X-Group pottery was found in the nearby test-pit that reached bedrock 2.95m below the general excavation level of 160cm in Locus 10. Both the radiocarbon date and the pottery date could have been related to earlier apparently residual material as well as to later material. Similarly, the same test-pit gave Beta-72854 that calibrated to 1218–895BC and supported the early date suggested by the presence of Napatan pottery (possibly as early as c.720BC), although Roman and X-Group pottery was also present at a slightly higher level. Finally, Beta-72855 gave a calibrated date of 89BC–AD330, comparable with a pottery date of AD100–200 (Table 1) and indicating at least a Meroitic origin for the base of the deposits in Locus 12, which also yielded Roman pottery.

Except for the indications of Napatan and Roman activity already mentioned, the structural sequence at Site 1037 appears to belong mainly to the Meroitic, X-Group and Early Christian periods, with no Classic Christian and only a trace of Late Christian to Islamic periods (Figs 30 and 31). Earlier evidence is probably residual, not associated directly with any part of the excavated structures. The earliest Meroitic activity consisted of the dumping of refuse in a crypt in Locus 12, an area that appears to have been an open yard possibly entered from the south and which produced the bulk of the organic evidence found at the site. Loci 2–11 consisted of rooms apparently constructed later during the Meroitic and/or X-Group periods, although some of the dating is uncertain. Later still was activity in Loci 2 and 5 during the Early Christian period, and crypts cut into earlier deposits in Locus 3 are probably also of that date (Figs 17 and 18). However, as already stated, the structural sequence at Site 1037 is characterized by continued activity, in spite of apparent cultural changes. It is also likely that the deposits within the loci are later in date than the walls, floors and other structural features of which the loci consist.

Houses excavated during other seasons at Qasr Ibrim had features that compared with some of those at Site 1037. For instance, deeper deposits contained indications of Roman and possibly earlier occupation. There were also similar structural features such as steps to upper levels, crypts (storage pits) dug into floors, stone sills and door jambs, blocked doorways, the use of both stone and mud-brick as building material, frequent re-flooring, plaster and whitewash on wall surfaces, and the presence of middens containing most of the artefactual material (W.Y. Adams 1996; 2013; Adams and Adams 2010). As with Site 1037, some houses also showed evidence of numerous structural changes over a long period, House 178, for instance, having 'the longest history of any dwelling at Qasr Ibrim, extending from Meroitic to Late Christian 2 times' (Adams and Adams 2010: 15; 17, Fig. 3). House 214 (formerly X–19) was also an example of a house modified numerous times (Plumley et al. 1977: 34; Adams and

Adams 2013: 39–40). Furthermore: 'Structures attributable to the earlier Ballaña period reflect a continuity of occupation from the preceding Meroitic period' (Adams and Adams 2013: 41). It seems, therefore, that other houses of a similar date to 1037 also had evidence of occupational continuity, in spite of comparably complex stratification. However, their publication (Adams and Adams 2010; 2013) tended to emphasize interpretation of the stratified evidence, rather than presenting an analysis of the data on which the interpretation was based, as has been attempted for 1037.

Other comparable houses at Qasr Ibrim were also similar to 1037 in that: 'Only a minority [of artefacts] were found in what could be considered culturally meaningful contexts, on house floors or buried in caches below them' (Adams and Adams 2010: 63). In addition, as seems also to have been the case at 1037, the quality of house construction at Qasr Ibrim declined during the Ballaña period: 'The earlier buildings … were very regular in plan and stoutly built. Some were certainly of Meroitic origin, though in most cases considerably modified in the Ballaña period … Later structures were noticeably more irregular in plan, and with generally thinner walls' (Adams and Adams 2013: 29).

Concerning the three sets of stone steps excavated at 1037, in Loci 3, 5 and 10, these might have given access to an upper storey of the building, as Adams and Adams (2013: 29) suggested for at least three Ballaña houses. However, they could have been necessary merely because the sloping character of the 1037 house-site resulted in a stepped structure rather than one with an upper floor. Adams and Adams (2013: 29) also commented on the general absence of fireplaces and the scarcity of grinding equipment and cooking pots in Ballaña houses at Qasr Ibrim, suggesting that the inhabitants lived mainly in a village on the riverbank and that the Ibrim structures were principally used for manufacturing and commercial purposes. Possibly this was because of a lack of water at Qasr Ibrim, so that it had to be carried up from the Nile far below. Alternatively, if some of the Ibrim houses did have upper floors, these might have provided living space while the ground floors were used for work-related activities but the provision of water could still have been a problem. Sanitation could also have been inadequate, although Site 1037 produced possible evidence of two latrines, one entered from Locus 5 and the other in the small Locus 8. A cesspit that would have been beneath a latrine was found in House 208, belonging to the Ballaña, Early Christian 1 and 2, and Classic Christian phases (Adams and Adams 2010: 18) but such facilities do not appear to have been common at Qasr Ibrim.

6

Artefacts Recorded from the 1986 Excavation of
House 1037

As a result of the dry conditions that existed for so long at Qasr Ibrim, 'the yield of artefactual finds ... is nothing short of prodigious, far exceeding that from any other habitation site in the Nile Valley' (Adams and Adams 2013: 10). Indeed, the excavation of Site 1037 showed that artefacts, including those of organic materials, could also survive after the flooding of deposits (such as in Locus 12) because of the anaerobic conditions produced by the saturation of those deposits. The artefactual assemblage from 1037 reflects the details of life at Qasr Ibrim, particularly during the Ballaña and Early Christian periods. Concerning the former period, that is most represented by the excavated evidence, Adams and Adams (2013: 19) have observed: 'Uniquely among known Ballaña settlements ... Qasr Ibrim was not a farming village but a commercial and to some extent a manufacturing centre. At least two export industries were attested: cotton spinning and wood turning ... Ibrim was in addition a major religious centre and a focus of pilgrimage'.

The following list has been compiled from Artefact Index Cards that were hand-written on-site by the Excavation Recorder or an assistant, of which photocopies were made available to the excavator (GC) soon after the completion of the 1986 excavation season. Occasionally the handwriting or the quality of the copies was uncertain and entries on the below list have been based on the most probable reading of the record. See Table 2 for a summary of this list but it should be noted that the material categories could only be approximately quantified, because they are based on the numbers of Artefact Index Cards rather than on numbers of artefacts or fragments of artefacts. In addition, not all materials are recorded on the cards, and some cards might be missing. Unstratified material is excluded and explanatory information about entries in the list are as follows: MD=Maximum Dimension. MDiam=Maximum Diameter. Entries with more than one artefact give the Maximum Dimension or the Maximum Diameter of the largest item. Artefacts listed as glass and faience are of glass unless otherwise indicated, because of uncertain identification of faience. Artefacts are grouped by provenance in each locus, and depths are within the 1986 excavated deposit. Surface artefacts within specified loci are treated as stratified; artefacts from the area around or within House 1037 but not within a specified locus are treated as unstratified. Numbers at the left margin of this list are unique Day Numbers, consisting of the date of excavation and the artefact number. 'REG. NO.' (Registration

Table 2. Site 1037: Distribution of material categories from Artefact Index Cards (or accessed from photographic records)

Artefact categories	Locus 1	Locus 2	Locus 3	Locus 4	Locus 5	Locus 6	Locus 7	Locus 8	Locus 9	Locus 10	Locus 11	Locus 12	Totals	%
Pottery	1	22	2	5	0	4	4	0	0	13	1	22	74	21.9
Copper/bronze	2	3	2	4	0	1	4	1	0	2	0	8	27	8.0
Iron	0	3	2	6	0	2	0	0	0	1	0	3	17	5.0
Glass & faience	4	8	8	13	4	4	9	4	4	23	2	36	119	35.0
Wood & ivory	0	4	0	2	0	0	1	3	0	5	0	18	33	10.0
Bone & horn	0	0	0	0	0	0	0	0	0	1	0	2	3	1.0
Stone	0	4	4	4	1	0	3	2	0	7	0	19	44	13.0
Miscellaneous	1	4	0	3	0	0	0	1	0	3	0	9	21	6.2
Totals	**8**	**48**	**18**	**37**	**5**	**11**	**21**	**11**	**4**	**55**	**3**	**117**	**338**	**100.1**

Only photocopies of the Index Cards were available; some were indistinct and some ambiguous.

Some Index Cards contain multiple artefacts or fragments of artefacts but cards are only counted once.

Mixed materials are counted as the main material present.

Index Cards for leather, textile, basketry and rope could not be accessed and some cards for materials listed might be missing.

Many of the artefacts are mentioned in Adams and Adams (2010; 2013) but discrepancies exist.

Number) is given when present in the records but is absent for most artefacts. Four entries in this list have neither Day Numbers nor Registration Numbers (three amphorae sherds, a stone lintel, a basket, and a rope) because they were accessed from the photographic records, not from the Artefact Index Cards on which they were not recorded. The Artefact Index Cards on which most of this list is based included only selected artefacts of pottery but all those of copper and bronze, iron, glass and faience, wood and ivory, bone and horn, stone, and miscellaneous artefacts. Textiles, basketry, leather, and other organic evidence were recorded separately and are usually not listed here because the relevant records were not available to the authors. Many of the artefacts in this list are also included in Adams and Adams (2010; 2013). Where this is the case, the entry here is annotated 'A&A 2010 [or 2013]' followed by the page number and/ or plate number. Furthermore, in a letter of 11 August 1986, Peter French, the Registrar for the 1986 excavation at Qasr Ibrim, kindly provided information about the date of some artefacts. Where an item could be identified in our list of the stratified items from the Artefact Index Cards, his opinion of the relevant date for the object follows the initials PF.

The pottery chronology and pottery ware descriptions in the following list are based on Adams (1986).

Locus 1: Street
(In the excavation field records this was called 'Street 1'.)

Pottery

86.1.4/31. Gaming counter cut from sherd. MDiam 3.9cm. 0–40cm.

Copper and bronze

86.1.2/37. Fragment of spindle hook? MD 1.8cm. 0–40cm.

86.1.4/39. Staple? MD 2.7cm. 0–40cm.

Iron

Nil.

Glass and faience

86.1.4/32. Bead. Diameter 0.6cm. 0–40cm.

86.1.4/30. Two fragments of vessels. MD 1.7cm. 0–40 cm. A&A 2013: 189, where given Day Number of 86.1.14.30. Also A&A 2013: 225, where (erroneously) listed as from the Isis Shrine.

86.1.2/36. Two beads, one glass, one faience? MD 1.1cm. 0–40cm.

86.1.2/26. Fragment of vessel. MD 1.5cm. 0–40cm.

Wood and ivory

Nil.

Bone and horn

Nil.

Stone

Nil.

Miscellaneous

86.1.4/33. Fragment of platter. Clay. Ware 'H1' type. MD 7.0cm. 0–40cm.

Locus 2: Room

Pottery

85.12.31/25. Fragment animal figurine. MD 4.9cm. West part of locus. 0–30cm (and surface?).

85.12.31/26. Fragment of unidentified object. Ware H18. MD 9.5cm. West part of locus. 0–30cm (and surface?).

85.12.31/14. Fragment horse figurine. MD 7.5cm. West part of locus. 0–30cm. A&A 2010: 303, where listed as Early Christian 2. Also A&A 2013: 213 and A&A 2013: 229, where (erroneously) listed as from the Isis Shrine.

86.1.6/15. Gaming counter. MD 2.5cm. West part of locus. 0–30cm. A&A 2010: 306, where listed as Early Christian 2. Also A&A 2013: 215, and A&A 2013: 229 where (erroneously) listed as from the Isis Shrine.

86.1.6/16. Two fragments figurines. Early Christian. MD 10.1cm. West part of locus. 0–30cm. A&A 2010: 304, where listed as two animal figurines and as Early Christian 2. Also listed twice in A&A 2013: 213 and 214, where described as female? figurine in the first entry and animal figurine in the second entry. (PF dated these approximately X-Group.)

86.1.1/34. Jar. Ware R1. Form approx D50. Style NIIA. MDiam 14.2. West part of locus. 0–30cm (Registration Number 86/30, only in our records). A&A 2010: 269, where described (erroneously?) as footed bowl and listed as Early Christian 2. Also A&A 2013: 175. Omitted from A&A 2013: 224, where (erroneously) confused with 86.1.1/33, which see.

86.2.5/12. Lamp. MD 9.7cm. 0–40cm below Early Christian floor (Registration Number 86/722). A&A 2010: 272, where listed as XC2. Also listed in A&A 2010: 292. (PF dated this 4th–6th century AD.)

86.2.5/15. Lamp, iron chain? X-Group. Ware R1. Form approximately P13. Style I. MD 10.7cm. Test-pit 0–40cm (Registration Number 86/723 only in our records). A&A 2013: 183.

86.2.13/7. Censer? Meroitic? Ware H1? Style X. MDiam 9.2. Test-pit 0–40cm (Registration Number 86/49).

86.1.1/15. Fragment horse figurine. MD 8.5cm. West part of locus. 30–60cm. A&A 2010: 303, where listed as Early Christian 2. Also A&A 2013: 213 and A&A 2013: 229, where (erroneously) listed as from the Isis Shrine. (PF dated this approximately X-Group.)

86.1.1/30. Bowl. Ware W2. Form C28. Style V. MDiam 11.6cm. West part of locus. 30–60cm (Registration Number 86/23). A&A 2010: 269, where listed as Early Christian 2.

86.1.1/31. Bowl. Ware W2. Form D71. Style V. MDiam 14.5cm. West part of locus. 30–60cm (Registration Number 86/21). A&A 2010: 270, where listed as Early Christian 2.

86.1.1/44. Fragments of female and animal figurines. MD 6.5cm. West part of locus. 30–60cm (Registration Number 86/709). A&A 2010: 303, where listed as female figurine and as Early Christian 2. Also A&A 2013: 213, and A&A 2013: 229 where listed as horse figurine in both places, and (erroneously) listed as Locus 4 (as also in A&A 2013: 213) and as from the Isis Shrine. (PF dated these approximately X-Group.)

86.1.2/18. Fragment of horse figurine. MD 8.7cm. West part of locus. 30–60cm. A&A 2013: 213. Also A&A 2013: 229, where (erroneously) listed as from the Isis Shrine. (PF dated this approximately X-Group.)

86.1.1/37. Spouted pot. Ware R10. Form G42. Style R10. MD 17.5cm (Fig. 32). West part locus. 30–60cm (Registration Number 86/36, only in our records). A&A 2010: 271, where listed as Early Christian 2. Also A&A 2013: 179, and A&A 2013: 224, where (erroneously) listed as from the Isis Shrine.

86.1.4/36. Incised sherd, depicts building? Ware R32. MD 13.0cm. West part of locus. 60–90cm (Registration Number 86/704).

86.1.1/33. Bowl. Ware W2. Form B1, MDiam 11.6cm. Style V (Fig. 33). West part of locus 60–90cm (Registration Number 86/12, only in our records, where (erroneously) described as a jar). A&A 2010: 268, where described as a goblet and listed as Early Christian 2. Also A&A 2013: 224, where (erroneously) listed as found in the Isis Shrine, and (erroneously) given the Day Number 86.1.1/34, which see.

86.1.4/13. Lamp. Ware W2. Form P17, loop handle. Style II. MDiam 9.9cm (Fig. 34). Pots in west part of locus 60–90cm (Registration Number 86/725). A&A 2010: 293 (errors: not Site 1027, not Registration Number 86/724), where listed as Early Christian 2. Also listed in A&A 2010: 272, with above errors. This lamp is of a type dated to Early Christian and Classic Christian 1 (Adams and Adams 2010: 148, Fig. 34).

86.1.5/23. Fragment of incense burner? MD 10.0cm. West part of locus. 90–120cm. A&A 2010: 302, where listed as Early Christian 2.

86.1.5/24. Fragment of figurine? MD 6.1cm. West part of locus. 90–120cm. A&A 2010: 304, where listed as Early Christian 2.

Fig. 32. Spouted pot. Ware R10. Form G42. Style R10. Height 17.5cm. From 30–60cm in west part of Locus 2, a stratigraphic context dated by its contained pottery to EC2, AD750–850 (Day Number 86.1.1/37, Registration Number 86/36). Photograph by Tony Bonner.

— Amphorae sherds in situ, north-west part of Locus 2, 31 December 1985 (Fig. 35). Pottery of this type was imported from Egypt during late Meroitic to Early Christian periods (A&A 2010: 85, Plate 7e, 86; 2013: 246, Plate 13a).

86.1.6/17. Fragment of tray. MD 9.1cm. West part of locus. 90–120cm. A&A 2010: 292, where listed as basin fragment and as Early Christian 2.

Copper and bronze

86.2.5/3. Fragment of pin/needle. MD 6.8cm. 0–40cm below Early Christian floor level (Registration Number 86/880).

86.2.5/4. Arrowhead. MD 4.9cm. 0–40cm below Early Christian floor level (Registration Number 86/924). A&A 2013: 201. Also A&A 2013: 227, where (erroneously) listed as from the Isis Shrine.

86.2.5/17. Inscribed base, Coptic? MDiam 1.9cm. Test-pit 0–40cm (Registration Number 86/875).

Fig. 33. Bowl, Ware W2, Form B1, Style V, Maximum Diameter 11.6cm. From a depth of 60–90cm in the west part of Locus 2, a stratigraphic context dated by its contained pottery to EC2, AD750–850 (Day Number 86.1.1/33, Registration Number 86/12). Photograph by Tony Bonner.

Fig. 34. Pottery lamp. Ware W2. Form P17 with loop handle. Style II. Maximum diameter 9.9cm. From group of pots at 60–90cm in west part of Locus 2, a stratigraphic context dated by its contained pottery to EC2, AD750–850 (Day Number 86.1.4/13, Registration Number 86/725). Photograph by Tony Bonner.

Fig. 35. Broken pots in situ in the north-west part of Locus 2, 31 December 1985. These are amphorae, imported to Nubia from Egypt during the late Meroitic to Early Christian periods (Adams and Adams 2010: 85, Plate 7e, 86; 2013: 246, Plate 13a). Scale in 1-cm divisions. Photograph by Tony Bonner.

Iron

86.2.5/1. Fragment of basketry needle. MD 7.0cm. 0–40 below Early Christian floor level.

86.1.1/11. Fragment of nail. MD 4.3cm. West part of locus. 30–60cm. A&A 2010: 286, where listed as Early Christian 2. Also A&A 2013: 205 and A&A 2013: 228, where (erroneously) listed as from the Isis Shrine.

86.1.4/12. Nail. MD 5.2cm. West part of locus. 60–90cm. A&A 2010: 286, where listed as Early Christian 2. Also A&A 2013: 205 and A&A 2013: 228, where (erroneously) listed as from the Isis Shrine.

Glass and faience

86.1.4/5. Bead. MD 1.5cm. Top of stone wall between Loci 2 and 10. Surface.

85.12.30/10. Bead. MD 0.6cm. West part of locus. 0–30cm. A&A 2010: 300 (with error), where listed as Early Christian 2.

86.1.1/13. Fragment of vessel. MD 2.9cm. West part of locus. 30–60cm. A&A 2010: 276, where listed as Early Christian 2. Also A&A 2013: 189 and A&A 2013: 225, where listed as bowl and (erroneously) as from the Isis Shrine.

86.1.1/12. Two beads. MDiam 0.9cm. West part of locus. 30–60cm. A&A 2010: 300, where listed as Early Christian 2. Also A&A 2013: 208 and A&A 2013: 228, where (erroneously) listed as from the Isis Shrine.

86.1.4/6. Bead. MD 1.0cm. West part of locus. 60–90cm. A&A 2010: 300, where listed as Early Christian 2.

86.2.5/7. Three fragments of vessels. MD 7.5cm. 0–40cm below Early Christian floor level. A&A 2010: 276, where listed as XC 2.

86.2.5/11. Two fragments of vessels. MD 4.2cm. Test-pit 0–40cm.

86.2.6/2. Fragment of bracelet. MD 2.7cm. Test-pit 40–80cm.

Wood and ivory.

86.2.5/14. Fragment of wood, furniture/structural? MD 14.7cm. 0–40cm below Early Christian floor level. A&A 2010: 313, where described as plank fragment and listed as XC2.

86.2.5/16. Furniture/screen part, probably ivory. MD 8.6cm. 0–40cm below Early Christian floor level (Registration Number 86/1120). A&A 2010: 291, where listed as wooden baluster and XC 2.

86.2.5/21. Plaque, probably ivory, probably of Hercules (Fig. 36). 0–40cm below Early Christian floor level (Registration Number 86/730). A&A 2010: 290, where listed as casket inlay and as XC 2? Also A&A 2013: 217, where (erroneously) listed as Locus 3, and A&A 2013: 230, where (erroneously) listed as from the Isis Shrine. (PF dated this Roman—X-Group.) Probably identifiable as Hercules because it depicts a muscular male figure with a club in the right hand, but an object in the left hand is unidentifiable as also is that between the legs. Possibly originally painted but no evidence survived of this.

86.2.6/30. Spindle whorl and fragment of spindle, both wood. Diameter 4.0cm. Test-pit 40–80cm.

Bone and horn

Nil.

Stone

85.12.31/4. Black granite rubbing stone. MD 11.4cm. West part of locus. 0–30cm. A&A 2010: 266, where listed as Early Christian 2.

86.1.1/14. Red granite pounder. MD 5.9cm. West part of locus. 30–60cm. A&A 2010: 266, where listed as Early Christian 2. Also A&A 2013: 161 and A&A 2013: 223, where (erroneously) listed as from the Isis Shrine.

86.1.4/11. Ironstone nodule. Amulet? Diameter 3.5cm. West part of locus. 60–90cm. A&A 2010: 307, where listed as natural nodule and Early Christian 2.

86.1.5/16. Fragment of pounder, chert. MDiam 6.5cm. West part of locus. 90–120cm. A&A 2010:266, where listed as Early Christian 2.

Fig. 36. Plaque probably ivory, probably of Hercules. From a depth of 0–40cm below an Early Christian floor level in the south-west corner of Locus 2, a stratigraphic context dated by its contained pottery to XC2, AD600–650, that gave a radiocarbon date (on wood) of cal AD71–426 (Table 1). (See Adams and Adams 2013: 217, where it is listed as a 'decorated plaque' of 'ivory'.) Scale in 1-cm divisions (Registration Number 86/730). Photograph by Tony Bonner.

Miscellaneous

86.2.5/5. Fragment of unidentified object. Clay. MD 3.2cm. 0–40cm below Early Christian floor level. A&A 2010: 304, where described as fish figurine? and listed as XC2.

86.1.2/19. Brush. Palm fibre. MD 17cm. West part of locus. 30–60cm. A&A 2013: 204. Also A&A 2013: 228, where (erroneously) listed as from the Isis Shrine.

86.1.2/41. Three fragments of vessels. Mud. MD 17.0cm. West part of locus. 30–60cm. A&A 2013: 188. Also A&A 2013: 224, where (erroneously) listed as from the Isis Shrine.

86.1.4/37. Unidentified object. Lightly fired clay. MDiam 8.0cm. West part of locus. 60–90cm. A&A 2010: 285, where described as ceramic weight and listed as Early Christian 2.

Locus 3: Room (East & West)

Pottery

86.1.28/20. Fragment of spindle whorl. Diameter 4.4cm. 0–40cm and surface.

86.2.1/28. Ostrakon, Greek? Ware H3. MD 5.6cm. West part of locus. 40–80cm (Registration Number 86/694). (PF confirmed the inscription as Greek.)

Copper and bronze

86.2.1/4. Fragment of sheet. MD 2.3cm. Surface and 0–40 cm.

86.2.6/23. Fragment of sheet. MD 1.8cm. Defining structures in east part of locus.

Iron

86.1.21/2. Nail. MD 8.6cm. 0–40cm.

86.2.6/10. Needle. MD 10.8cm. East part of locus (Registration Number 86/878). A&A 2013: 195. Also A&A 2013: 226, where (erroneously) listed as from the Isis Shrine.

Glass and faience

86.1.26/1. Two fragments of bracelets. MD 4.0cm. Surface and 0–40cm.

86.1.26/2. Four fragments of vessels. MD 2.4cm. Surface and 0–40cm.

86.1.26/3. Two beads. MD 3.5cm. Surface and 0–40cm.

86.2.1/7. Three fragments of vessels. MD 1.9cm. Surface and 0–40cm.

86.1.21/1. Fragment of vessel. MD 2.3cm. 0–40cm.

86.2.6/4. Fragment of vessel. MD 2.0cm. Removal of crypts, east part of locus.

86.2.6/3. Fragment of bead, faience. MDiam 1.5cm. Removal of crypts, east part of locus.

86.2.6/24. Two fragments of vessels. MD 1.7cm. Defining structures in east part of locus.

Wood and ivory

Nil.

Bone and horn

Nil.

Stone

86.1.23/8. Fragment of grinding stone. Sandstone. MD 15.5cm. Surface and 0–40cm.

86.2.2/26. Two sandstone blocks, hieroglyphs on one, covered in whitewash. MD 33cm. West part of locus 0–40cm.

86.2.6/33. Fragment of sandstone column. MD 34cm. West part of locus, over fifth step down.

86.2.6/34. Pestle? Sandstone. MD 6.0cm. Defining structures in east part of locus (Registration Number 86/1051).

Miscellaneous

Nil.

Locus 4: Room

Pottery

85.12.26/38. Fragment of smoking pipe. MD 3.7cm. Locus 4 and east edge of area. Surface.

86.1.27/26. Gaming counter from sherd. MDiam 3.1cm. Doorway and common wall, Loci 4–9.

86.1.29/8. Ostrakon, Coptic? Black ink. Ware R30. MD 9.2cm. Fill over rubble spill, Loci 4–9 (Registration Number 86/684).

86.1.6/13. Jar, Ware R32, Form W13, Style I. MD 34.2cm (Fig. 37). Depth about 50cm (Registration Number 86/58, only in our records). A&A 2013:186. Also A&A 2013: 224, where (erroneously) listed as from the Isis Shrine.

86.1.1/21. Gaming counter from sherd. MD 3.7cm. 50–80cm below top of west wall. A&A 2013: 215. Also A&A 2013: 229, where (erroneously) listed as from the Isis Shrine.

Copper and bronze

85.12.26/7. Cosmetic implement, complete. MD 8.9cm. Surface below water-borne deposits (Registration Number 86/904).

85.12.26/22. Cosmetic implement, complete. MD 14.5cm. Surface below water-borne deposits (Registration Number 86/899).

86.1.1/25. Finger-ring? MDiam 1.8cm. 50–80cm below top of west wall (Registration Number 86/910). A&A 2013: 209. Also A&A 2013: 229, where (erroneously) listed as from the Isis Shrine.

86.1.1/52. Broken human figurine. MD 4.6cm. 50–80cm below top of west wall (Registration Number 86/853). A&A 2013: 213, Plate 53c, where described in caption as (Roman soldier?). Also A&A 2013: 229, where (erroneously) listed as from the Isis Shrine. (PF dated this Roman—X-Group.)

Iron

86.1.27/30. Object of sheet. MD 6.6cm. Doorway and wall between Loci 4 and 9.

86.2.1/21. Nail. MD 5.5cm. South part of fill.

86.1.1/8. Fragment of wire. MD 2.7cm. 50–80cm below top of west wall.

Fig. 37. Jar from about 50cm depth in south-west corner of Locus 4, a stratigraphic context dated by its contained pottery to X, AD400–550 (but with a low sherd count, the latest sherds being X). Ware R32, Form W13, Style I; see W.Y. Adams 1986: 444, 447, 450, 455–6, where these attributes are classified as Meroitic. Scale in 1-cm divisions (Day Number 86.1.6/13, Registration Number 86/58). Photograph by Tony Bonner.

86.1.1/24. Loop. MDiam 2.6cm. 50–80cm below top of west wall (Registration Number 86/909). A&A 2013: 199.

85.12.31/20. Nail. MD 7.7cm. Pit 1.

85.12.31/21. Two unidentified objects. Figure 38 shows one: MD 11cm. Pit 1 (Registration Number 86/862).

Glass and faience

85.12.26/6. Bead. Diameter 0.4cm. Surface beneath water-borne deposits.

86.1.25/2. Fragment of vessel. MD 1.7cm. Doorway blocking between Loci 4 and 9.

86.1.25/17. Bead, faience. MD 0.9cm. Doorway blocking between Loci 4 and 9.

86.1.27/10. Fragment of vessel. MD 1.3cm. Doorway and wall between Loci 4 and 9.

86.1.27/11. Bead. Diameter 0.5cm. Doorway and wall between Loci 4 and 9.

Fig. 38. Unidentified iron object, possibly part of a harness. From fill of Pit 1 (a crypt fragment) in Locus 4, a stratigraphic context dated by its contained pottery to X1, AD400–500 (Day Number 85.12.31/21, Registration Number 86/862). Scale in 1-cm divisions. Photograph by Tony Bonner.

85.12.31/3. Bead. Diameter 0.4cm. Outside Locus 4, South-West corner. 50–75cm defining mud wall.

86.1.1/10. Five beads. MD 0.8cm. South part of locus. 50–80cm below top of west wall. A&A 2013: 208, where they are (erroneously?) listed as 86.1.1/20. Also A&A 2013: 228, where (erroneously) listed as from the Isis Shrine.

86.1.1/9. Four fragments of vessels. MD 3.0cm. South part of locus. 50–80cm below top of west wall. A&A 2013: 189, where (erroneously) given Day Number of 86.1.1/19. Also listed (erroneously) under this number in A&A 2013: 225 and (erroneously) listed as from the Isis Shrine.

86.1.26/7. Three beads. MD 1.1cm. Lower fill 1.

86.1.26/8. Three fragments of vessels. MD 2.2cm. Lower fill 1.

86.2.3/7. Two fragments of vessels. MD 2.4cm. South-West part of locus. Rubble and fill.

85.12.31/19. Two beads. MDiam 0.7cm. Pit 1 fill.

85.12.31/18. Fragment of bracelet. MD 1.0cm. Pit 1 fill. (PF identified this as Islamic.)

Wood and ivory

85.12.26/37. Fragment of wooden spindle whorl. Diameter 4.5cm. Locus and east edge of locus. Surface.

86.1.29/9. Fragment of wooden lid. Diameter 6.7cm. Fill over rubble spill. Loci 4–9.

Bone and horn

Nil.

Stone

85.12.26/24. Fragment of sandstone disc, with hole. Diameter 2.4cm. Locus and east edge of locus. Surface.

85.12.30/29. Fragment of sandstone bowl. MD 5.3cm. Surface and top of deposit.

86.2.3/14. Two joining fragments of offering-table. Sandstone. MD 54.5cm. 1984 test-pit side. A&A 2013: 210. Also A&A 2013: 221, where (erroneously) listed as from the Isis Shrine.

86.2.3/13. Fragment of grindstone. Sandstone. MD 62cm. 1984 test-pit side.

Miscellaneous

85.12.26/29. Coil, round-section lead bar. MD 21.0cm. Locus and east edge of locus. Surface.

85.12.26/30. Small loop, lead. Diameter 1.5cm. Locus and east edge of locus. Surface.

85.12.26/36. Bead. Shell pierced for stringing. MD 1.5cm. Locus and east edge of locus. Surface.

Locus 5: Room

Pottery

Nil.

Copper and bronze

Nil.

Iron

Nil.

Glass and faience

85.12.28/2. Bead. Diameter 0.4cm. North-west part of locus. 0–40cm. A&A 2010: 300, where listed as Early Christian 1.

85.12.28/1. Fragment of vessel. MD 1.1cm. North-west part of locus. 0–40cm. A&A 2010: 277, where listed as Early Christian 1.

86.1.6/6. Bead. Diameter 0.5cm. North-east and central west part of locus. 80–110cm. A&A 2010: 300, where listed as Early Christian 2.

86.1.7/45. Bead, faience? MD 0.4cm. North-east and central west part of locus. 80–110cm. A&A 2010: 300 (error: not Locus 2), where listed as Early Christian 2.

Wood and ivory

Nil.

Bone and horn

Nil.

Stone

85.12.28/17. Fragment of quartzite, probably from vessel. MD 3.0cm. North-west part of locus. 20–60cm. A&A 2010: 266, where listed as (alabaster?) bowl rim fragment and Early Christian 1.

Miscellaneous

Nil.

Locus 6: Room

Pottery

85.12.30/2. Ostrakon, sherd, Meroitic on exterior and interior (Figs 39 and 40). East part of locus, 0–30cm (Registration Number 86/675). (PF dated Meroitic—X-Group.)

Fig. 39. Ostrakon. Exterior surface of sherd with parts of five lines of Meroitic script in black ink. From a depth of 0–30cm in the eastern part of the fill of Locus 6, a stratigraphic context dated by its contained pottery to X2, AD500–550 (Table 1). Scale in 1-cm divisions (Day Number 85.12.30/2, Registration Number 86/675). Photograph by Tony Bonner.

Fig. 40. Ostrakon. Interior surface of same sherd as Fig. 39 with parts of two lines of Meroitic script in black ink. Details as for Fig. 39.

86.1.15/39. Jar, Meroitic. Ware R32. Form W2. Style I. MD 39.2cm (Fig. 41). East part of locus, 30–60cm (Registration Number 86/59, only in our records). A&A 2013: 186. Also A&A 2013: 224, where (erroneously) listed as from the Isis Shrine.

86.1.1/36. Bowl. Ware R32. Form approximately D47. Style I. MDiam 18.3cm. East part of locus, 30–60cm (Registration Number 86/37, only in our records). A&A 2013: 177. Also A&A 2013: 224, where (erroneously) listed as from the Isis Shrine, and Ware recorded as R30.

86.1.8/24. Two gaming counters from sherds. MDiam 3.1cm. 90–120cm.

Copper and bronze

85.12.30/35. Illegible coin. MDiam 1.4cm. 0–30cm (Registration Number 86/946). A&A 2013: 229. Also A&A 2013: 214, where Day Number is given (erroneously) as 85.12.30 (as also in A&A 2013: 229). (PF dated this apparently Islamic?)

Iron

86.2.13/9. Fragment of sheet. MD 7.6cm. East part of locus. 60–90cm.

Fig. 41. Meroitic jar, Ware R32. Form W2, Style I (Day Number 86.1.15/39, Registration Number 86/59). In situ with a grindstone fragment and perforated sherds from a colander in east part of Locus 6, 30–60cm, a stratigraphic context dated by its contained pottery to X1/X2, AD400–550, 30 December 1985. Scale in 1-cm divisions. Photograph by Tony Bonner.

85.12.31/8. Piece of heavy plate. MD 7.1cm. East part of locus. 60–90cm. A&A 2013: 217, where (erroneously) given a Day Number of 85.12.3/8. Also A&A 2013: 230, where (erroneously) listed as from the Isis Shrine.

Glass and faience

85.12.30/21. Three fragments of vessels. MD 4.1cm. East part of locus. 0–30cm. A&A 2013: 189. Also A&A 2013: 225, where (erroneously) listed as from the Isis Shrine.

85.12.31/2. Bead. MD 0.9cm. East part of locus. 30–60cm.

85.12.30/1. Bead. Diameter 0.5cm. East part of locus. 30–60cm.

86.1.8/2. Fragment of vessel. MD 1.9cm. 90–120cm.

Wood and ivory

Nil.

Bone and horn

Nil.

Stone

Nil.

Miscellaneous

Nil.

Locus 7: Room

Pottery

86.1.2/31. Lid. Ware R25. Form Q6. Style I. MDiam 8.3cm. 0–40cm (Registration Number 86/53, only in our records). A&A 2013: 184. Also A&A 2013: 224, where (erroneously) listed as from the Isis Shrine.

85.12.29/5. Gaming counter from sherd. Ware PD4 Plain. MDiam 4.0cm. East part of locus. 0-40cm.

86.1.1/32. Bowl. Ware R30. Form D11a. Style X. MDiam 10.4cm. East part of locus. 0–40cm (Registration Number 86/20, only in our records). A&A 2013: 174. Also A&A 2013: 224, where (erroneously) listed as from the Isis Shrine.

86.1.1/22. Bowl. Ware W29. Form approximately B16/D11a. Style II. MDiam 10.7cm (Fig. 42). 0–40cm (Registration Number 86/18, only in our records). A&A 2013: 178. Also A&A 2013: 224, where (erroneously) listed as from the Isis Shrine.

Copper and bronze

85.12.29/11. Fragment of needle? MD 5.7cm. East part of locus. 0–40cm. A&A 2013: 195. Also A&A 2013: 226, where (erroneously) listed as from the Isis Shrine.

85.12.29/12. Two fragments of sheet. MD 4.0cm. East part of locus. 0–40cm.

86.1.2/35. Three fragments of sheet plus rivets (and iron washers). MD 6.0cm. 0–40cm. A&A 2013: 230, where (erroneously) listed as from the Isis Shrine, and (erroneously) given Day Number 86.2.1/35.

Fig. 42. Bowl, Ware W29. Form approximately B16/D11a. Style II. Maximum diameter 10.7cm. From a depth of 0–40cm in Locus 7, a stratigraphic context dated by its contained pottery to MX/X1, AD350–500 (Day Number 86.1.1/22, Registration Number 86/18). Photograph by Tony Bonner.

85.12.29/13. Flat arrowhead of sheet. MD 2.9cm (Fig. 43). East part of locus. 0–40cm (Registration number 86/926). A&A 2013: 201, where described as iron. Also A&A 2013: 227, where described as iron and (erroneously) listed as from the Isis Shrine.

Iron

Nil.

Glass and faience

86.1.2/30. Two fragments of vessels. MD 2.5cm. 0–40cm. A&A 2013: 189. Also A&A 2013: 225, where (erroneously) listed as from the Isis Shrine.

86.1.2/29. Fragment of multicoloured slab, inlay? MD 2.0cm. 0–40cm. (PF dated this probably X-Group?)

86.1.2/28. Bead. Diameter 0.4cm. 0–40cm.

86.1.1/7. Knob? MD 1.6cm. 0–40cm (Registration number 86/736).

86.1.1/6. Fragment of vessel. MD 3.9cm. 0–40cm. A&A 2013: 189, where (erroneously) given Day Number of 86.1.1/16. Also listed (erroneously) under this number in A&A 2013: 225 and (erroneously) listed as from the Isis Shrine.

85.12.31/31. Fragment of unidentified object. MD 0.9cm. East part of locus. 0–40cm.

85.12.31/30. Fragment of bead. Diameter 0.7cm. East part of locus. 0–40cm.

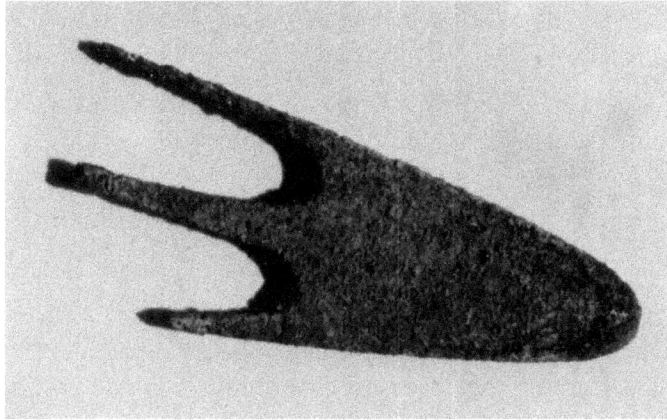

Fig. 43. Flat arrowhead of copper/bronze sheet. Maximum dimension 2.9cm. From 0–40cm in east part of Locus 7, a stratigraphic context dated by its contained pottery to MX/X1, AD350–500 (Day Number 85.12.29/13, Registration Number 86/926). Photograph by Tony Bonner.

85.12.31/23. Fragment of vessel. MD 2.0cm. East part of locus. 0–40cm. A&A 2013: 189. Also A&A 2013: 225, where (erroneously) listed as from the Isis Shrine.

85.12.29/10. Fragment of bead. Diameter 0.95cm. East part of locus. 0–40cm.

Wood and ivory

85.12.31/29. Wooden spindle whorl. Diameter 3.7cm. East part of locus. 0–40cm. A&A 2013: 226, where (erroneously) listed as from the Isis Shrine.

Bone and horn

Nil.

Stone

86.1.1/35. Three rubbing stones. Black granite? MD 33cm. 0–40cm. A&A 2013: 199. Also A&A 2013: 227, where (erroneously) listed as from the Isis Shrine.

86.1.2/34. Unidentified object. Sandstone. MD 5.4cm. 0–40cm. A&A 2013: 217. Also A&A 2013: 230, where (erroneously) listed as from the Isis Shrine.

86.1.1/1. Grinder. Black granite. MD 9.2cm (Fig. 44). 0–40cm. A&A 2013: 161. Also A&A 2013: 223, where (erroneously) listed as from the Isis Shrine.

Miscellaneous

Nil.

Locus 8: Room

Pottery

Nil.

Fig. 44. Grinder of black granite. Maximum dimension 9.2cm. From 0–40cm in fill of Locus 7, a stratigraphic context dated by its contained pottery to MX/X1, AD350–500 (Day Number 86.1.1/1, Registration Number not recorded). Photograph by Tony Bonner.

Copper and bronze

86.1.4/38. Fragment of sheet in tube shape. MD 2.8cm. 0–30cm.

Iron

Nil.

Glass and faience

86.1.4/34. Fragment of vessel base. MDiam 5.3cm. 0–30cm. A&A 2013: 189. Also A&A 2013: 225, where listed as bowl and (erroneously) as from the Isis Shrine.

86.1.2/27. Fragment of vessel (bottle). Diameter 1.7cm. 0–30cm.

86.1.2/25. Bead. Diameter 0.5cm. 0–30cm.

86.1.7/4. Bead. Diameter 0.6cm. Fill to 30cm below top of stonework.

Wood and ivory

86.1.7/39. Two spindle whorls, wood (Fig. 45). Fill to 30cm below top of stonework. A&A 2013: 197, where recorded as wood + gold. Also A&A 2013: 226, where (erroneously) listed as from the Isis Shrine.

86.1.8/17. Worked wood. MD 47.2cm. West part of locus. 30cm below top of stonework.

Fig. 45. Two lathe-turned wooden spindle whorls. From Locus 8, fill to 30cm below top of stonework, a stratigraphic context dated by its pottery content to MX, AD350–400 (Day Number 86.1.7/39, Registration Number not recorded). Scale in 1-cm divisions. Photograph by Tony Bonner.

86.1.8/16. Worked wood. MD 48.5cm. West part of locus. 30–60cm below top of stonework.

Bone and horn

Nil.

Stone

86.1.4/35. Ball. Ironstone? Diameter 3.5cm. 0–30cm (Registration Number 86/916).

86.1.7/12. Ball. Ironstone. Missile? Diameter 2.4cm. 0–30cm below top of stonework.

Miscellaneous

86.1.7/33. Loom-weight. Clay. MD 14.8cm. West part of locus. 0–30cm below top of stonework. A&A 2013: 198, where described as mud. Also A&A 2013: 227, where (erroneously) listed as from the Isis Shrine. (PF dated this Early Christian or earlier.)

Locus 9: Room

Pottery

Nil.

Copper and bronze

Nil.

Iron

Nil.

Glass and faience

86.1.4/3. Bead. Diameter 0.5cm. 0–40cm below top of east wall.

86.1.2/16. Three beads, 2 glass, 1 faience? MDiam 0.8cm. 0–40cm below top of east wall. A&A 2013: 208. Also A&A 2013: 228, where (erroneously) listed as from the Isis Shrine.

86.1.2/15. Fragment of vessel, faience. MD 1.3cm. 0–40cm below top of east wall. A&A 2013: 188. Also A&A 2013: 224, where (erroneously) listed as from the Isis Shrine.

86.1.2/14. Two fragments of vessels. MD 3.4cm. 0–40cm below top of east wall. A&A 2013: 189, where given the Day Number of 86.1.12/14. Also A&A 2013: 225, where (erroneously) listed as from the Isis Shrine.

Wood and ivory

Nil.

Bone and horn

Nil.

Stone

Nil.

Miscellaneous

Nil.

Locus 10: Room

Pottery

86.1.14/28. Gaming counter from sherd. Ware H1. MDiam 2.4cm. West part of locus and west of locus. 40–80cm. A&A 2013: 215. Also A&A 2013: 230, where (erroneously) listed as from the Isis Shrine.

86.1.15/23. Footed bowl. Ware R1. Form D11. Style NIIA. MDiam 18.9cm. West part of locus and west of locus. 40–80cm (Registration Number 86/29, only in our records). A&A 2013: 175. Also A&A 2013: 224, where (erroneously) listed as from the Isis Shrine.

86.1.15/29. Footed bowl, X-Group. Ware R25. Form D14a. Style I. MDiam 14.7cm. West part of locus and west of locus. 40–80cm (Registration Number 86/24, only in our records). A&A 2013: 177. Also A&A 2013: 224, where (erroneously) listed as from the Isis Shrine.

86.1.15/30. Bowl, X-Group. Ware R25. Form C46. Style I. MDiam 15.5cm. West part of locus and west of locus. 40–80cm (Registration Number 86/4, only in our records). A&A 2013: 174. Also A&A 2013: 178 and A&A 2013: 224, where (erroneously) listed as from the Isis Shrine.

86.1.15/43. Lamp? X-Group. Ware H1. Form approximately P23. Style X. MDiam 5.5cm. West part of locus and west of locus. 40–80cm (Registration Number 86/52, only in our records). A&A 2013: 182.

86.1.19/11. Footed bowl. Ware W29. Form DIIA. Style II. MDiam 10.7cm. 0–40cm below top of north wall (Registration Number 86/19, only in our records). A&A 2013: 178. Also A&A 2013: 224, where (erroneously) listed as from the Isis Shrine.

86.1.20/11. Spindle whorl from sherd. Ware R1. MDiam 3.9cm. 0–40cm below top of north wall.

86.1.28/7. Bowl, X-Group. Ware R25. Form C46. Style I. MDiam 15.2cm. 0–40cm below top of north wall (Registration Number 86/5, only in our records). A&A 2013: 174. Also A&A 2013: 224, where (erroneously) listed as from the Isis Shrine.

86.1.28/6. Footed bowl, X-Group. Ware W29. Form D14a. Style V. MDiam 12.2cm. 80–120cm below top of north wall (Registration Number 86/14, only in our records). A&A 2013: 178. Also A&A 2013: 224, where (erroneously) listed as from the Isis Shrine.

86.1.28/8. Footed bowl, X-Group. Ware R25. Form D14a. Style I. MDiam 13.2cm. 80–120cm below top of north wall (Registration Number 86/26, only in our records). A&A 2013: 177. Also A&A 2013: 224, where (erroneously) listed as from the Isis Shrine.

86.1.28/9. Bowl, X-Group. Ware R25. Form C46. Style I. MDiam 15.8cm. 80–120cm below top of north wall (Registration Number 86/2 only in our records). A&A 2013: 174. Also A&A 2013: 224, where (erroneously) listed as from the Isis Shrine.

86.2.1/29. Meroitic ostrakon, sherd. Ware H4. Black ink. MD 5.4cm. 120–160cm below top of north wall (Registration Number 86/697). (PF dated this Meroitic—X-Group.)

86.2.8/18. Gaming counter from sherd. Ware R32? MDiam 3.0cm. Test-pit 2.0m to bedrock. A&A 2013: 215. Also A&A 2013: 230, where (erroneously) listed as from the Isis Shrine.

Copper and bronze

86.1.21/29. Fragment of cosmetic tool? MD 5.5cm. 0–40cm below top of north wall.

86.2.5/2. Fragment of sheet. MD 3.2cm. 120–160 cm below top of north wall.

Iron

86.1.7/29. Fragment of nail? MD 3.5cm. West part of locus and west of locus. 0–40cm.

Glass and faience

86.1.4/19. Four fragments of vessels. MD 5.4cm. West part of locus and west of locus. Surface and 0–40cm. A&A 2013: 189. Also A&A 2013: 225, where (erroneously) listed as from the Isis Shrine.

86.1.4/18. Beads, 1 glass, 1 faience. MD 0.5cm. West part of locus and west of locus. Surface and 0–40cm.

86.1.7/30. Amulet? Miniature jug. MD 2.3cm. West part of locus and west of locus. 0–40cm (Registration Number 86/735).

86.1.7/22. Beads, 1 glass, 1 faience. MDiam 0.5cm. West part of locus and west of locus. 0–40cm.

86.1.7/21. Three fragments of vessels. MD 3.4cm. West part of locus and west of locus. 0–40cm.

86.1.7/20. Fragment of bracelet. MD 1.3cm. West part of locus and west of locus. 0–40cm.

86.1.6/27. Fragment of vessel. MD 1.8cm. West part of locus and west of locus. 0–40cm.

86.1.14/23. Glass residue. MD 0.7cm. West part of locus and west of locus. 40–80cm.

86.1.12/9. Bead fragment, faience. MD 1.0cm. West part of locus and west of locus. 40–80cm.

86.1.25/10. Two beads. MDiam 0.45cm. 40–80cm below top of north wall.

86.1.25/11. Fragment of vessel. MD 2.8cm. 40–80cm below top of north wall.

86.1.26/6. Three fragments of vessels. MD 4.2cm. 80–120cm below top of north wall.

86.1.27/22. Two beads. MDiam 0.7cm. 80–120cm below top of north wall.

86.1.27/23. Fragment of bracelet. MD 2.2cm. 80–120cm below top of north wall.

86.1.27/24. Two fragments of vessels. MD 3.5cm. 80–120cm below top of north wall.

86.1.27/25. Fragment of unidentified object, faience? MD 1.6cm. 80–120cm below top of north wall.

86.2.5/6. Bead. Diameter 0.8cm. 120–160cm below top of north wall.

86.2.5/8. Fragment of bracelet. MD 3.2cm. 120–160cm below top of north wall.

86.2.5/9. Four fragments of vessels. MD 2.6cm. 120–160cm below top of north wall.

86.2.5/10. Fragment of slab, inlay? MD 3.3cm. 120–160cm below top of north wall. (PF dated this probably X-Group?)

86.2.5/20. Fragment of bead/amulet, gold and figure. MD 2.3cm. 120–160cm below top of north wall (Registration Number 86/741). A&A 2013: 209, where described as (faience? pendant?). Also A&A 2013: 229, where (erroneously) listed as from the Isis Shrine.

86.2.3/9. Three fragments of good quality glass vessel. MD of largest piece is 13.0 cm (Fig. 46). 120–160cm below top of north wall (Registration Number 86/738).

86.2.6/1. Bead. MD 1.0cm. Decorated with gold. Test-pit 0–75cm.

Fig. 46. Three fragments of a good quality glass vessel. Maximum dimension of largest piece is 13.0cm. From 120–160cm below top of north wall in Locus 10, a stratigraphic context dated by its contained pottery to X1, AD400–500, that gave a radiocarbon date (on wood) of cal 352BC–AD132 (Table 1) (Day Number 86.2.3/9, Registration Number 86/738). Photograph by Tony Bonner.

Wood and ivory

86.1.18/16. Fragment of knob for iron key, wood. MD 7.0cm. 0–40cm below top of north wall (Registration Number 86/784). (PF dated this Roman—X-Group.)

86.1.21/15. Fragment of spindle? Wood. MD 18.4cm. 0–40cm below top of north wall.

86.1.30/33. Fragment of unidentified wooden object. MD 3.8cm. 80–120cm below top of north wall.

86.2.5/18. Bowl of wooden spoon. MD 10.4cm. 120–160cm below top of north wall. A&A 2013: 162. Also A&A 2013: 223, where (erroneously) listed as from the Isis Shrine.

86.2.6/32. Fragment of wood. Furniture or screen. MD 6.3cm. Test-pit 0–75cm (Registration Number 86/1121).

Bone and horn

86.1.14/38. Fragment of handle? Bone. MD 4.7cm. West part of locus and west of locus. 40–80cm (Registration Number 86/1045, but not in our records). A&A 2013: 218, where listed as long bone piece. Also A&A 2013: 231, where (erroneously) listed as from the Isis Shrine.

Stone

—. Sandstone lintel, Meroitic inscription, from 1984 surface of Locus 10 (Fig. 47).

Fig. 47. Sandstone lintel after removal from the 1984 excavated surface of Locus 10 (Fig. 12). Inscribed in Meroitic, with three representations of Meroitic offering-tables, largely obliterated by pounding. It probably fell from above the blocked doorway between Locus 2 and Locus 10, suggesting the existence of a high-status doorway during Meroitic times. The attempted obliteration of its religious symbols is likely to have been during the Early Christian period, in order to remove evidence of pagan beliefs. Probably at a later date, when the lintel had already fallen, it was used for sharpening metal tools. Scale in 1-cm divisions (Day and Registration Numbers not recorded). Photographs by Tony Bonner, 1986, digitally manipulated by Andrew Stawowczyk Long.

86.1.4/20. Spindle whorl? Sandstone. Diameter 2.6cm. West part of locus and west of locus. Surface and 0–40cm. A&A 2013: 197. Also A&A 2013: 226, where (erroneously) listed as from the Isis Shrine.

86.1.4/21. Flint flake. MD 3.4cm. West part of locus and west of locus. Surface and 0–40cm.

86.1.6/26. Fragment of vessel/lamp? Steatite, part oil-coated. MD 2.4cm. West part of locus and west of locus. 0–40cm.

86.1.19/15. Three fragments of grindstones. Sandstone. MD 42cm. 0–40cm below top of north wall.

86.1.30/27. Fragment of grindstone. Sandstone. MD 31.5cm. 80–120cm below top of north wall.

86.2.6/20. Two fragments of pounders? Quartzite, sandstone. MD 6.3cm. Test-pit 75–200cm.

Miscellaneous

85.12.19/26. Pot-stand. Cotton cloth, X-Group. Diam 13cm. 80–120cm below top of west wall (Registration Number 86/560 PART). A&A 2013: 203, where Registration Number is given as 86/80. Also A&A 2013: 228, where (erroneously) listed as from the Isis Shrine.

86.2.6/12. Votive object? Clay. MD 3.6cm. 120–160cm below top of north wall (Registration Number 86/1099).

86.2.8/14. Fragment of human figurine? Clay. MD 3.4cm. Test-pit 2m to bedrock.

Locus 11: Room

Pottery

86.2.4/19. Gaming counter from sherd. Ware H2 Plain. MDiam 3.3cm. West, upper fill and surface.

Copper and bronze

Nil.

Iron

Nil.

Glass and faience

86.2.4/20. Eight fragments of vessels. MD 4.0cm. West part of locus. Upper fill.

86.2.9/1. Four beads, including 1 faience? MDiam 0.6cm. West part of locus. Upper fill.

Wood and ivory

Nil.

Bone and horn

Nil.

Stone

Nil.

Miscellaneous

Nil.

Locus 12: Open space
(In the excavation field records this was called 'Area South of Room 5')

Pottery

86.1.9/23. Fragment of offering tray. Ware H25. MD 15.0cm. Level 1. (PF dated this probably X-Group.)

86.1.14/34. Fragment of offering tray. Ware H25. Style I. MD 7.1cm. Level 1. A&A 2013: 210. Also A&A 2013: 222, where (erroneously) listed as from the Isis Shrine. (PF dated this probably X-Group.)

86.1.14/35. Two gaming counters from sherds. Ware R25 and R32. MDiam 3.3cm. Level 1. A&A 2013: 215, where listed as one disc. Also A&A 2013: 230, where (erroneously) listed as from the Isis Shrine.

86.1.15/22. Lamp. Ware R32? Style I. MDiam 9.7cm. Level 1 (Registration Number 86/720).

86.1.15/27. Footed bowl, Meroitic. Ware R32. Form approx D28. Style I. MDiam 13.0cm. Level 1 (Registration Number 86/27).

86.1.9/22. Meroitic ostrakon, sherd. Ware R30. Black ink. MD 3.1cm. Level 1 (Registration Number 86/699). (PF dated this Meroitic—X-Group.)

86.1.9/6. Two gaming counters from sherds. MD 2.6cm. Level 1. A&A 2013: 215. Also A&A 2013: 230, where (erroneously) listed as from the Isis Shrine.

86.1.21/16. Gaming counter from sherd. MDiam 3.2cm. Level 1. A&A 2013: 215. Also A&A 2013: 230, where (erroneously) listed as from the Isis Shrine.

86.1.21/7. Gaming counter from sherd. MDiam 2.0cm. Level 1. A&A 2013: 215. Also A&A 2013: 230, where (erroneously) listed as from the Isis Shrine.

86.1.18/6. Gaming counter from sherd. MDiam 2.1cm. Level 1. A&A 2013: 215. Also A&A 2013: 230, where (erroneously) listed as from the Isis Shrine.

86.1.18/12. Three gaming counters from sherds. One is Ware R32. MDiam 2.9cm. Level 1. A&A 2013: 215, where listed as one disc. Also A&A 2013: 230, where (erroneously) listed as from the Isis Shrine.

86.1.15/36. Gaming counter from sherd. MDiam 2.9cm. Level 1.

86.1.15/37. Beaker, Meroitic. Ware R30. Form D3. Style X. MD 5.0cm. Level 1 (Registration Number 86/51).

86.1.5/8. Meroitic ostrakon, sherd. Ware R32. Black ink. MD 8.8cm. 0–40cm (Registration Number 86/672). (PF dated this Meroitic—X-Group.)

86.1.6/21. Gaming counter from sherd. Ware R32. MDiam 3.8cm. 0–40cm. A&A 2013: 215. Also A&A 2013: 229, and 230 where (erroneously) listed as from the Isis Shrine, and (erroneously) listed with Day Number 86.1.21/6.

86.1.8/6. Gaming counter from sherd. Ware R32? Diameter 2.7cm. Surface below 40cm. A&A 2013: 215. Also A&A 2013: 229 where (erroneously) listed as from the Isis Shrine.

86.1.8/35. Ostrakon, sherd. Ware R30. Black ink. MD 6.8cm. Surface below 40cm (Registration Number 86/686). (PF identified the inscription as Greek or Coptic, dated Roman—Early Christian.)

86.1.8/22. Gaming counter from sherd. Ware R32. MDiam 2.7cm. Surface below 40cm.

86.1.8/13. Two joining frags of pottery lamp. Ware R32. MD 8.9cm. Surface below 40cm.

86.1.23/6. Gaming counter from sherd. Ware R32. MDiam 2.6cm. Level 2. A&A 2013: 215.

86.1.29/2. Gaming counter from sherd. Ware R32. MDiam 2.7cm. Level 5: north feature. A&A 2013: 215. Also A&A 2013: 230, where (erroneously) listed as from the Isis Shrine.

86.2.2/19. Fragment of vessel. Ware: highly polished. MDiam 3.8cm. Level 6: north feature.

Copper and bronze

86.1.6/36. Arrowhead, chisel end, single barb. MD 5.8cm. 0–40cm (Registration Number 86/923).

86.1.6/37. Ring, fragment of bar attached. MD 3.2cm. 0–40cm (Registration Number 86/896).

86.1.6/41. Fragment of sheet. MD 6.2cm. 0–40cm.

86.1.7/27. Fragment of sheet. MD 2.2cm. 0–40cm.

86.1.9/14. Two fragments of sheet. MD 1.9cm. Level 1.

86.1.9/1. Two fragments of sheet. MD 3.5cm. Surface below 40cm.

86.1.8/9. Fragment of sheet. MD 1.5cm. Surface below 40cm.

86.1.8/10. Fragment of sheet. MD 2.4cm. Surface below 40cm.

Iron

86.1.6/34. Tweezers. MD 6.2cm. 0–40cm (Registration Number 86/894). A&A 2013: 200. Also A&A 2013: 227, where (erroneously) listed as from the Isis Shrine.

86.1.7/28. Fragment of sheet. MD 3.2cm. 0–40cm.

86.1.9/15. Hook. MD 2.5cm. Level 1.

Glass and faience

86.1.12/4. Six fragments of vessels. MD 2.1cm. Level 1.

86.1.12/5. Fragment of bracelet. MD 1.7cm. Level 1.

86.1.13/11. Three fragments of vessels. MD 3.5cm. Level 1.

86.1.13/24. Three fragments of slab. MD 6.7cm. Level 1. (PF dated this probably X-Group?)

86.1.14/9. Fragment of vessel. MD 2.1cm. Level 1.

86.1.14/10. Bead. MD 0.7cm. Level 1.

86.1.15/2. Three fragments of vessels. MD 3.0cm. Level 1.

86.1.16/4. Fragment of vessel. MD 2.3cm. Level 1.

86.1.18/5. Two fragments of vessels. MD 5.2cm. Level 1.

86.1.20/4. Fragment of bracelet. MD 1.5cm. Level 1.

86.1.20/5. Fragment of vessel. MD 2.7cm. Level 1.

86.1.20/13. Fragment of vessel. MD 1.2cm. Level 1.

86.1.21/4. Bead. Diameter 0.3cm. Level 1.

86.1.21/19. Six fragments of vessels. MD 3.5cm. Level 1.

86.1.22/8. Two fragments of vessels. MD 2.6cm. Level 1.

86.1.9/9. Five beads, glass, green stone, faience. MD 1.2cm. Level 1.

86.1.9/7. Six fragments of vessels. MD 2.1cm. Level 1.

86.1.23/3. Two fragments of vessels. MD 2.1cm. Level 2. Terrace wall foundation trench fill.

86.1.23/4. Two beads. MDiam 0.5cm. Level 2. Terrace wall foundation trench fill.

86.1.26/4. Bead. Diameter 0.5cm. Level 3.

86.1.27/4. Fragment of bead, faience. MD 0.9cm. Level 3.

86.1.26/5. Four fragments of vessels. MD 2.2cm. Level 3.

86.1.27/5. Two fragments of vessels. MD 2.7cm. Level 3.

86.1.27/9. Fragment of bracelet. MD 1.0cm. Level 4. Fill of south feature.

86.1.28/21. Fragment of bracelet. MD 3.2cm. Level 5. Fill of north feature.

86.2.1/16. Base of vessel. MDiam 4.5cm. Level 5. Fill of north feature, west half.

86.1.7/25. Fragment of bracelet? MD 0.7cm. Level 0–40cm.

86.1.7/24. Five fragments of slab, inlay? MD 4.5cm. Level 0–40cm. (PF dated this probably X-Group?)

86.1.7/23. 11 fragments of vessels. MD 6.2cm. Level 0–40cm.

86.1.6/30. Seven fragments of vessels. MD 4.3cm. Level 0–40cm.

86.1.6/20. Two fragments of vessel, that join. MD 3.8cm. Level 0–40cm.

86.1.5/22. Three beads. MD 0.8cm. Level 0–40cm.

86.1.5/15. Five fragments of vessels. MD 3.6cm. Level 0–40cm.

86.1.8/4. Eight fragments of vessels. MD 5.2cm. Surface below 40cm.

86.1.8/3. Bead. Diameter 0.35cm. Surface below 40cm.

86.1.9/2. Three fragments of vessels. MD 2.9cm. Surface below 40cm.

Wood and ivory

86.1.9/16. Fragment of pin? Wood. MD 6.0cm. Level 1.

86.1.20/19. Female figurine. Wood. MD 7.6cm (Fig. 48). Level 1 (Registration Number 86/769). A&A 2013: 213. Also A&A 2013: 229, where (erroneously) listed as from the Isis Shrine.

86.1.12/18. Wooden box. Diameter 4.5cm (Fig. 49). Level 1 (Registration Number 86/1105). A&A 2013: 190; 247, Plate 14d. Also A&A 2013: 225, where (erroneously) listed as from the Isis Shrine.

86.1.20/20. Fragment of wooden comb (Fig. 50). Level 1. Registration Number not recorded but Day Number 86.1.20/20 matches that in A&A 2013: 200. Also A&A 2013: 227, where (erroneously) listed as from the Isis Shrine. Adams and Adams (2010: 126) comment that: 'Wooden combs have been found in abundance at Qasr Ibrim'.

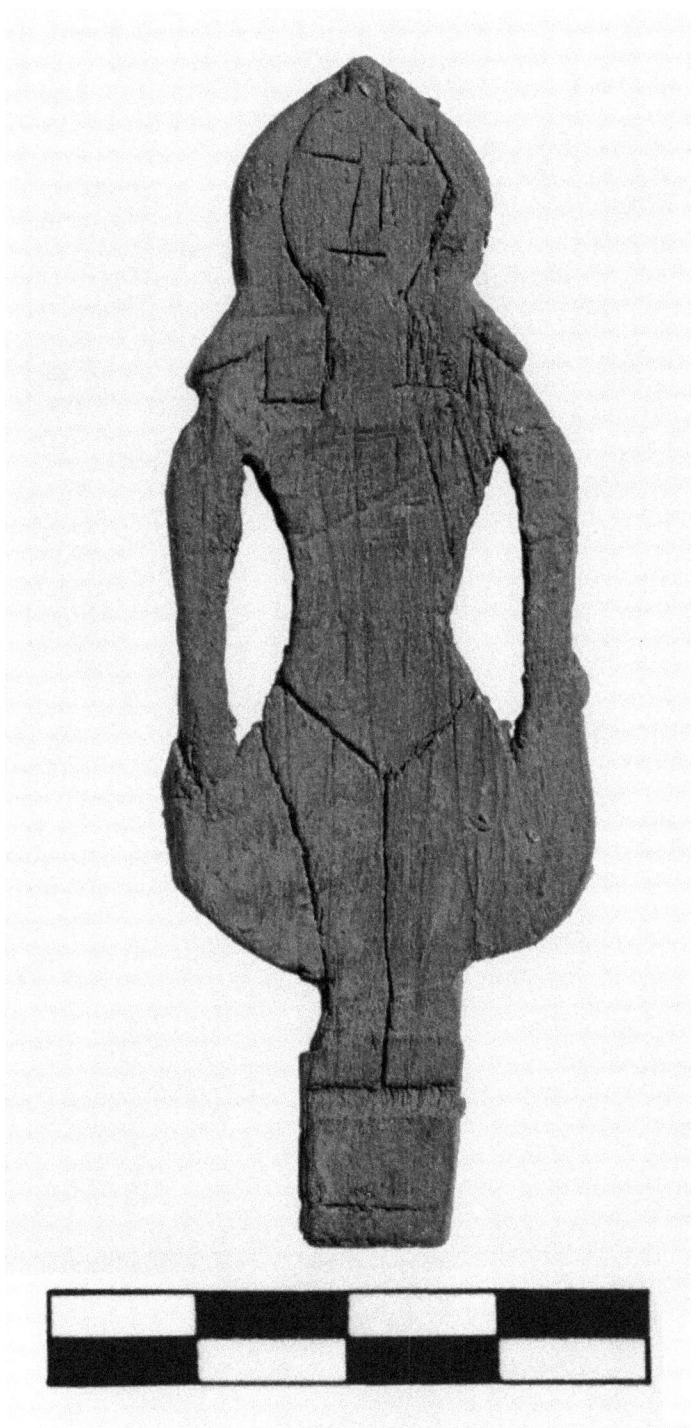

Fig. 48. Flat wooden carving of a female, found in Level 1 of Locus 12: carbonized material and soil, a stratigraphic context dated by its pottery content to M2, AD200–350, that gave a radiocarbon date (on wood) of cal AD130–531 (Table 1). (See Adams and Adams 2013: 213, where it is listed as a wooden 'female figurine'.). Scale in 1-cm divisions (Day Number 86.1.20/19, Registration Number 86/769). Photograph by Tony Bonner.

86.1.12/12. Wooden spindle whorl, inlayed. Diameter 3.6cm. Level 1 (Registration Number 86/760). A&A 2013: 197, Plate 22b, where described in caption as having four bone or ivory inlays. Also A&A 2013: 226, where (erroneously) listed as from the Isis Shrine.

86.1.12/17. Fragment of unidentified wooden object. MD 71cm. Furniture or structural? Level 1.

Fig. 49. Lathe-turned wooden box from the same context as Fig. 48 and of the same date. Diameter 4.5cm (Day Number 86.1.12/18, Registration Number 86/1105). (See also Adams and Adams 2013: 247, Plate 14d, and 190 where it is listed as a 'thin-walled box'.) Photograph by Tony Bonner.

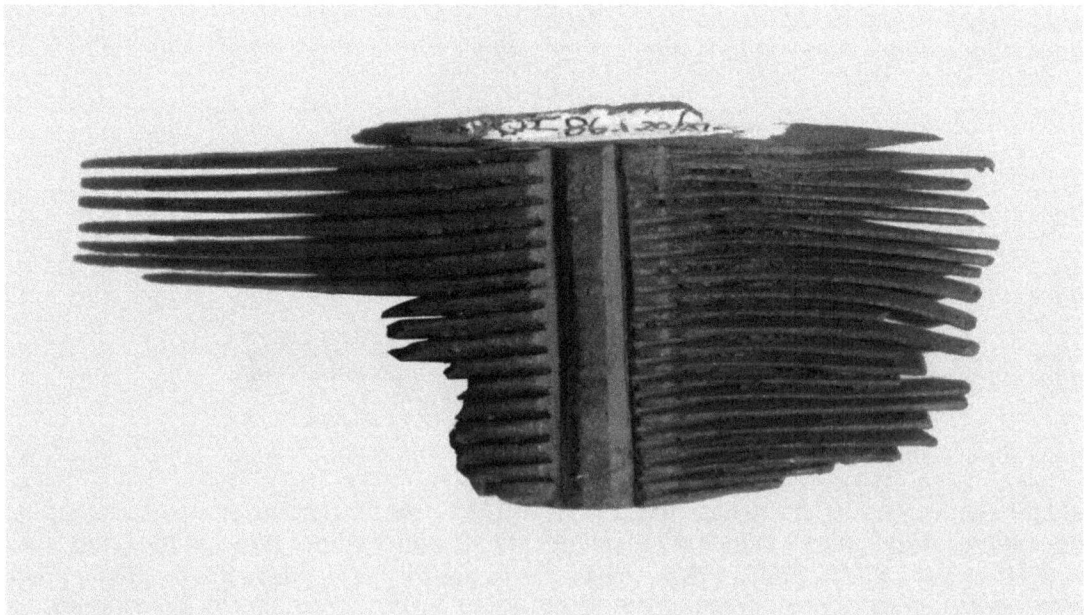

Fig. 50. Fragment of a wooden comb from the same context as Fig. 48 and of the same date. Measurements 5.7 by 2.6cm (Day Number 86.1.20/20, Registration Number not recorded). (See Adams and Adams 2013: 200, where it is listed as a wooden 'two-sided comb'.) Photograph by Tony Bonner.

86.1.13/22. Fragment of unidentified wooden object. MD 30cm. Level 1.

86.1.13/23. Fragment of wooden object. Archer's loose? Diameter 3.5cm. Level 1. A&A 2013: 218, where listed as thick ring. Also A&A 2013: 231, where (erroneously) listed as from the Isis Shrine.

86.1.13/36. Wooden peg. MD 25.3cm. Level 1.

86.1.14/31. Two joining fragments unidentified wooden object. MD 6.7cm. Level 1.

86.1.14/33. Two wooden unidentified objects. MD 10.0cm. Level 1.

86.1.15/54. Wooden spindle whorl. Diameter 3.4cm. Level 1. A&A 2013: 197. Also A&A 2013: 227, where (erroneously) listed as from the Isis Shrine.

86.1.21/27. Fragment of spindle whorl or lid? Wood, copper/bronze, and iron. MD 8.0cm. Level 1.

86.1.26/14. Fragment of wooden handle. MD 8.6cm. Level 3. A&A 2013:195. Also A&A 2013: 226, where (erroneously) listed as from the Isis Shrine.

86.1.27/32. Fragment of wooden bowl. MD 7.5cm. Level 4. Fill of south feature.

86.1.6/40. Two joining fragments unidentified wooden object. MD (together) 5.5cm. 0–40cm.

86.1.8/30. Fragment of key knob, wood. MD 7.1cm. Surface below 40cm (Registration Number 86/785). (PF dated this Roman—X-Group.)

86.1.8/38. Two spindle whorls, wood and iron. MDiam 3.6 cm. Surface below 40cm. A&A 2013: 197. Also A&A 2013: 226, where (erroneously) listed as from the Isis Shrine.

Bone and horn

86.2.1/22. Fragment of cow rib. Tool? MD 6.4cm. Level 1.

86.1.14/43. Horn disc, black. Gaming counter? MDiam 1.3cm. Level 1.

Stone

86.1.12/3. Pounder. Quartzite. MDiam 5.8cm. Level 1.

86.1.14/30. Unidentified object. Sandstone, triangular. MD 5.1cm. Level 1.

86.1.14/39. Sandstone disc with 2 drilled holes, button? Diameter 3.8cm. Level 1 (Registration Number 86/1045 PART). A&A 2013: 205.

86.1.15/1. Pounder. Red granite. MD 5.5cm. Level 1. A&A 2013: 161. Also A&A 2013: 223, where (erroneously) listed as from the Isis Shrine.

86.1.15/32. Sandstone weight, has hole with rope-wear marks from suspension. MD 27.6cm. Level 1. A&A 2013: 199. Also A&A 2013: 227, where (erroneously) listed as from the Isis Shrine.

86.1.15/33. Sandstone rubbing stone. MD 25.5cm. Level 1. A&A 2013: 199. Also A&A 2013: 227, where (erroneously) listed as from the Isis Shrine.

86.1.15/40. Red granite unidentified object, reused as rubbing stone? MD 41.5cm. Level 1.

86.1.22/17. Fragment of sandstone tray. MD 21.5cm. Level 1.

86.1.23/9. Sandstone ballista ball. MDiam 15.0cm. Level 2. Terrace wall foundation trench fill. A&A 2013: 202. Also A&A 2013: 227, where (erroneously) listed as from the Isis Shrine.

86.2.2/13. Pounder, chert? MDiam 6.8cm. Level 6. Fill of north feature.

86.2.2/25. Fragment of grindstone. Sandstone. MD 40cm. Level 6. Fill of north feature.

86.1.5/17. Fragment of rubbing stone. Sandstone. MD 13.5cm. 0–40cm.

86.1.6/22. Unidentified object. Sandstone. MD 4.0cm. 0–40cm.

86.1.6/23. Rubbing stone. Red granite. MD 64cm. 0–40cm. A&A 2013: 161, where no locus stated but must be Locus 12. Also A&A 2013: 223, where (erroneously) listed as from the Isis Shrine and given the (erroneous) Day Number of 76.1.6/23 (as also in A&A 2013: 161).

86.1.6/42. Five joining fragments of sandstone bowl. MD 14cm. 0–40cm. A&A 2013: 190. Also A&A 2013: 225, where no locus stated but must be Locus 12, and where (erroneously) listed as from the Isis Shrine.

86.1.7/10. Grinder. Red granite? MD 22.8cm. 0–40cm. A&A 2013: 199. Also A&A 2013: 227, where (erroneously) listed as from the Isis Shrine.

86.1.7/11. Lower grinding stone. Sandstone. MD 13.8cm. 0–40cm.

86.1.7/32. Fragment of vessel? Quartzite. MD 2.6cm. 0–40cm.

86.1.7/48. Pounder. Chert? MDiam 7.3cm. On burnt surface at 40cm.

Miscellaneous

—. Basket (Fig. 51). Level 1.

—. Length of rope (Fig. 52). Level 1.

85.12.19/21. Pot-stand. Horsehair and cotton cloth. Meroitic. Diameter 12cm. Level 1 (Registration Number 86/566 PART). A&A 2013:203. Also A&A 2013: 228, where (erroneously) listed as from the Isis Shrine.

Fig. 51. Basket from the same context as Fig. 48 and of the same date. Scale in 1-cm divisions (Day and Registration Numbers not recorded). Photograph by Tony Bonner.

Fig. 52. Rope, one end with a loop, the other end broken, in situ, 11 January 1986. From the same context as Fig. 48 and of the same date. Scale in 1-cm divisions (Day and Registration Numbers not recorded). Photograph by Tony Bonner.

86.1.13/32. Loom weights and fragments. Mud, palm fibre and cotton cloth. MD 18.5cm. Level 1. (PF dated these Early Christian or earlier.)

86.1.14/13. Jar sealing. Uninscribed. Clay. Diameter 7.7cm. Level 1.

86.1.15/44. Loom weight. Mud. MD 13cm. Level 1. A&A 2013: 227, where (erroneously) listed as from the Isis Shrine, and given Day Number of 86.1.17/44. (PF dated these Early Christian or earlier.)

86.1.7/26. Fragment of unidentified object. Lead. MD 3.0cm. 0–40cm.

86.1.8/23. Fragment of animal figurine. Lightly fired clay. MD 5.0cm. Surface below 40cm (Registration Number 86/1096). A&A 2013: 213, where described as horse figurine. Also A&A 2013: 229, where (erroneously) listed as from the Isis Shrine.

86.2.1/1. Fragment of bead. Carnelian. MD 1.0cm. Level 5: Fill of north feature, west half.

Analysis of Artefacts from the 1986 Excavation of House 1037

Adams and Adams (2010; 2013) listed the artefacts excavated from the Ballaña and Earlier Medieval periods at Qasr Ibrim according to their function, in the process demonstrating the great diversity of the overall artefactual evidence. In our investigation of the artefacts from Site 1037 we have instead listed the artefacts in their main material categories, in order to show their distribution across the twelve excavated loci of the site (Table 2), (Figs 12 and 13). It was impractical to examine the details of their *stratigraphic* distribution within the loci as a whole because of a lack of uniformity in the deposits in different parts of the site. Nevertheless, some artefactual patterning is apparent. Although Loci 1, 9, and 11 are excluded as too small in area to contribute to this, it can be seen that Loci 12 had by far the greater amount of artefactual evidence (117 out of 338 artefacts: 35 per cent). This was because it was a midden in which garbage had accumulated. Of the other loci, Locus 10 had 16 per cent, Locus 2 had 14 per cent, Locus 4 had 11 per cent, Locus 7 had 6 per cent, and Locus 3 had 5 per cent of the artefacts. The remaining two loci (6 and 8), although small in area, had 3 per cent each. Because of partial excavation in 1983–1984 (Alexander 1984a; 1984b), that had removed some of the deposits and their contents from five of the loci, it is uncertain how much of the artefactual evidence from Site 1037 reflects the patterning before that excavation. It appears that these five of the twelve loci discussed here were affected to varying extents in this way but the available field records are ambiguous concerning the details. The only part of the site of which it can be stated with certainty that it was totally unexcavated before 1986 was Locus 12. Unsatisfactory though this is as a means of providing information on the uses of the different loci, a comparison of the quantities of different material categories across the site does suggest some variation in activities between the loci. Thus glass and faience, the most numerous category, was present in all loci (35 percent of the artefacts) but iron in only half of them and represented by far fewer artefacts (only 5 per cent). Evidence for weaving, in the form of loom weights, was even less common, being present in only Locus 12, apparently disposed of amongst the garbage, and in Locus 8, thought to be a possible latrine. Taphonomic factors had also influenced such distribution, wood and ivory items being most numerous in Locus 12 but absent in half of the other loci in spite of the dry conditions of their deposits. However, the shallowness of several of the latter, compared to the depth of Locus 12 (Figs 28 and 29), also limited the number of artefacts that they contained.

The range of materials represented by the artefact assemblage suggests that most were of local origin, with the exception of some of the glass and faience of which high quality might indicate exotic origins, including some of the beads. Items of copper, bronze and iron might also have been imported from the north at times, as also would have been the case for pottery, which included amphorae for transporting wine or oil from Egypt (Fig. 35) although the bulk of the pottery was produced in Nubia (Figs 32–34 and 37). Objects of wood, ivory, bone and horn were most likely also local in origin, although the probable scarcity of wood in the Qasr Ibrim area would suggest that some of it could have come from elsewhere, probably by boat on the Nile. The miscellaneous artefact category also appears to reflect mainly local activities, only the presence of several lead objects in Loci 4 and 12 perhaps indicating an external source.

Particular artefacts from the site did provide useful information about chronology. Most important was a stone lintel inscribed in Meroitic, that had lain on the 1984 excavated surface of Locus 10 but had been removed to the stone magazine near the cathedral, where it was photographed by Tony Bonner in February 1986 (Figs 12 and 47). Unaccountably, no certain mention of it has been found in publications or unpublished records but Alexander (1984a: 11) contains the following comment: 'The year's most important finds will probably prove to be: (i) The meroitic inscriptions, which have increased the total corpus known by 10%. They include a dedication (on a probably temple lintel) by a King of Ibrim and the two longest inscriptions yet found anywhere.' Site 1037 was certainly not a temple but, if the quotation refers to the lintel from Locus 10, it is possible that this large and impressive stone had been recycled from a temple at Qasr Ibrim or that Alexander's comment was inaccurate. Certainly reuse of stone seems to have occurred in Site 1037, as is evident from a piece with hieroglyphs found in Locus 3 that had been covered in whitewash (86.2.2/26) and from other sculptured fragments (Connah 1986c: 210). However, an exact identification of the 1037 lintel must remain a problem. Because Meroitic inscriptions are still almost unreadable, the content of this one is unknown and it is not mentioned in Leclant *et al.* (2000). The lintel also had three representations of what appear to be Meroitic offering tables. However, an attempt had been made to obliterate the latter symbols by deliberate pounding and two areas of the lintel, which appeared to be of fine-grained sandstone, had also been used for sharpening metal tools. The lintel had lain close to a blocked doorway between Loci 2 and 10 (Fig. 12) and, with a weight possibly in excess of 100 kilograms, is most likely to have fallen from above the doorway rather than to have come from elsewhere. Its presence suggested the former existence of a high-status doorway during Meroitic times, and the obliteration of its religious symbols was probably done during the Early Christian period in an attempt to remove evidence of pagan beliefs. No attempted translation of its Meroitic inscription is known but it is interesting that this had not been deliberately damaged in spite of such attention to other features.

Another artefact of special chronological value is a Meroitic ostrakon (85.12.30/2), a potsherd of 9.5 by 6.2 centimetres that has parts of five lines of Meroitic script in black ink on its exterior

(Fig. 39) and parts of two more on its interior (Fig. 40), inscriptions that are not included in Leclant *et al.* (2000). It came from a depth of 0–30 centimetres in the eastern part of the fill of Locus 6, a stratigraphic context dated by its contained pottery to X2, AD500–550 (Table 1). Although possibly residual, it does provide a further indication of the Meroitic associations of this site. Six other ostraka were also found in Site 1037 (three in Meroitic (86.1.5/8, 86.1.9/22, and 86.2.1/29, that PF thought dated Meroitic—X-Group); one in Greek or Coptic (86.1.8/35, that PF thought dated Roman—Early Christian); one in Greek (86.2.1/28, that PF thought potentially dateable); and one possibly in Coptic (86.1.29/8, that PF did not comment on). Except for the ostrakon shown in Figures 39 and 40, no photographs were available of these other ostraka, but collectively the seven examples add some support to an overall date of Meroitic to X-Group and Early Christian for Site 1037. Also apparently Meroitic is a broken sandstone offering table from Locus 4 (86.2.3/14). Inscribed and decorated objects of this type are discussed and illustrated by Shinnie (1967: 113–14, Figs 35 and 36) and Geus (1991: 70, Fig. 14b), although the one from Site 1037 has no inscription or decoration. It appears to have been found low in the fill of the incomplete test-pit excavated by John Alexander in 1984 (Fig. 19). Its context was uncertain, although probably Meroitic according to associated pottery. However, Adams and Adams (2013: 210) listed it in the Ballaña Phase but without a Registration Number, although they gave the same Day Number of 86.2.3/14 that matches the Artefact Index Card.

A fourth item that is suggestive of a pre-Christian date is a plaque (Fig. 36) probably of ivory (86.2.5/21), that probably represents Hercules (PF dated this Roman—X-Group). It was possibly originally painted; although no evidence of this survived, the painting of ivory carvings has been recorded as early as the second millennium BC (Connor 1998: 3). This plaque came from a depth of 0–40 centimetres below an Early Christian floor level in the south-west corner of Locus 2, a stratigraphic context dated by its contained pottery to XC2, AD600–650, that has a radiocarbon date (on wood) of Beta–44131: cal AD71–426 (Table 1). Hercules was the subject of a minor religious cult in the Roman world (Lipka 2009: 62, 76, 168, 184). Also of special interest is a flat wooden carving (86.1.20/19) of a female figure (Fig. 48), found in Level 1 of Locus 12 that consisted of carbonized material and soil and was dated by its pottery content to M2, AD200–350, and by a radiocarbon date (on wood) of Beta–44132: cal AD130–531 (Table 1). This figurine was probably also a pre-Christian cult object, representing an apparently naked woman perhaps holding removed clothes. Anatomical details are limited but it is possible that they were painted onto the wood and are now lost. Female figurines (often painted) were found in Early and Classic Christian levels at Qasr Ibrim but seem to have been usually of ceramic (Adams and Adams 2010: 200), as also was the case at Meinarti, a site in northern Sudan with female figurines that were often painted (Adams 2000: 92, Fig. 30; Plate 20c). However, a comparable but cruder wooden figurine to that from Site 1037 does exist (Adams and Adams 2010: Plate 39d). It is from a much earlier excavation and has a Registration Number of 63/49. Significantly, it has a horizontal groove near its base, like the 1037 figurine, as if it was intended to be attached to some other object. Both the Hercules plaque and the female figurine from Site 1037 suggest that pagan beliefs were only gradually replaced by Christianity at Qasr Ibrim. As Dijkstra (2013: 114) has observed of the fourth century AD, 'there is a remarkable continuity of traditional cults and practices in northern Lower Nubia at this time'.

A further chronological contribution is provided by an almost illegible coin of copper or bronze (85.12.26/47) that came from an unstratified context in or adjacent to Locus 4 and is therefore not included in the above artefacts list (PF dated this to 4th–6th century AD). One surface artefact (85.12.26/38) from Locus 4 of Site 1037, and several unstratified artefacts from the vicinity of the site, consisted of fragments of Islamic smoking pipes, indicating later activity in the area, as did a stone wall of Islamic date that lay over the remains of Locus 3 on its east side (Fig. 18).

Locus 12 was particularly important because it consisted of a stratified midden deposit that had formed outside the building complex, in an open area that might have been used as an animal pen (Fig. 24). This was excavated as seven stratigraphic contexts (Table 1). It contained the most organic material found in Site 1037. At the time of the excavation it was damp and smelly, suggesting ancient use of the area as a latrine, but it was apparent that its condition was actually because the area of Site 1037 had been under 7 metres of water caused by high lake levels in Lake Nasser after 1970. These had fallen by the time of the excavation seasons of 1984 and 1986 (Alexander 1985: 21, Fig. 5) but this deposit had not dried out completely. Outstanding examples of the remarkable condition of preservation amongst organic artefacts, from this locus, included, a lathe-turned wooden box (Fig. 49), a fragment of a wooden comb (Fig. 50), a complete basket (Fig. 51) and a length of rope (Fig. 52). There were also many other organic items recovered from this midden deposit, showing that even after several years of the site's immersion in water such material had not been destroyed. However, by 2000 water had severely damaged most of Qasr Ibrim, either covering parts of the site or percolating into its deposits (Rose 2000: 2) but valuable organic evidence might still be preserved in contexts like Locus 12 in Site 1037 because of waterlogged, anaerobic conditions.

Amongst the numerous organic artefacts excavated from Site 1037 in 1986, textiles, basketry and leather were the most common. Comprehensive records of basketry and leather artefacts from the site were not available to the authors but their presence should not be overlooked, (Fig. 51 shows the remarkable preservation of basketry in part of 1037). Items of leather could also be particularly informative, as Veldmeijer (2013) has demonstrated for the Ottoman Period at Qasr Ibrim, but there is as yet no comparable detailed published study of leather from Meroitic or Ballaña contexts at this site (however see N.K. Adams 2013b: 115). As for that later period, valuable information could be provided about the use of this material, particularly for footwear.

The situation is much better for textiles. Nettie Adams, the textile analyst, kindly provided a report at Qasr Ibrim, dated 9 February 1986 and since published in part (N.K. Adams 1986), on the textiles from Site 1037 (both sources are used here). There were 600 textile fragments from fourteen provenances in 1037, which required 597 separate identifications (this in a context where 4732 specimens from Qasr Ibrim were analysed during the 1982 excavation season). Of those from Site 1037, 92 per cent were of cotton, 7 per cent were of flax, and there was a trace of wool. The midden deposit in Locus 12, Level 1, not surprisingly produced 76.5 per cent of the recovered textiles. Although the material was fragmentary, the fabric in many cases was surprisingly well preserved.

All of the major fabric types of the Meroitic period were represented in this collection. The bulk was plain weave of several kinds: very close, fine weave; loose, open weave; and a type with very tight spinning which had a hard rough texture. Half-basket (two wefts over one warp) and basket weave (two wefts over two warps) of various grades were found. Pile fabric was represented by a relatively large specimen of 39 by 44 centimetres. The last fabric type was one with multiple wefts, a textured cloth with a ribbed appearance. This occurred in flax, and was of Roman date or earlier.

All of the features of the weaving process (starting borders, selvedges and end borders) were present. The starting border was particularly valuable because it changed the interpretation of a certain fabric type from warp face to weft face. Although the openwork borders were not the only end border types found here, they were the most spectacular features of Meroitic textiles. Three examples were catalogued: 86T/125, 126, and 127.

The collection also provided fragmentary examples of Meroitic clothing: the most complete one probably worn as a skirt (86T/074) and measuring 59 by 90 centimetres. It had a narrow openwork border, the typical Meroitic decorative finish on garments. There were also two types of loin-cloth, one with a short decorative tie; a kilt with the remains of the usual embroidered decoration; a pendant apron, also with fragments of embroidery; and a garment of unknown use.

Collectively, the textile evidence was typical of waste from domestic occupation, with indications of small-scale household crafts particularly within a Meroitic context. Evidence that weaving was occurring in or near Site 1037 was provided by loom weights in Loci 8 and 12 of the above artefacts list (86.1.13/32, 86.1.15/44 and 86.1.7/33). Spindle whorls in Loci 2, 3, 4, 7, 8, 10 and 12 (86.2.6/30, 86.1.28/20, 85.12.26/37, 85.12.31/29, 86.1.7/39, 86.1.20/11, 86.1.4/20, 86.1.12/12, 86.1.15/54, 86.1.8/38 and 86.1.21/27 (possibly a lid)), indicate that spinning was also practised in the house, as indicated by spun thread found in Loci 10 and 12 (Connah 1986c: 86, 91, 109). Other information on textiles from Qasr Ibrim is available in W.Y. Adams (1996: 126); W.Y. Adams and N.K. Adams (2010: 156–191); N. K. Adams (2013a: 65–81) and N.K. Adams 2013b: 107–117).

Details of some artefactual and of ecofactual evidence were not recorded in the Artefact Index Cards or were not available to the authors of this book but have been accessed from GC's Field Notes (Connah 1986c). As often the case with field notes, these are not easy to use but the person who wrote them has interpreted them here. Textiles occurred in Loci 10 and 12 (Connah 1986c: 54, 102, 109, 116, 129, 175, 176, 236 and 237), often fragmentary but in one case 'a mass of cloth in several lots' (Connah 1986c: 86). There was also a complete bag made of basketry, covered with textile and leather, which was recovered from the west section of Locus 6, at 30 centimetres below the top of the section, on the last day of the excavation, 11 February 1986 (Connah 1986c: 241). The rope shown in Fig. 52 was the largest piece recovered but significant examples were also found in Loci 10 and 12 (Connah 1986c: 69, 86, 96, 97, 102, 214). Pieces of string occurred in Loci 2, 8, 10 and 12 (Connah 1986c: 38, 41, 47, 69, 70, 76, 92, 96, 97, 102, 116, 122, 129, 175, 176 and 203). Fig. 51 was a remarkably well-preserved basket from Locus 12 but basketry was common although some of it fragmentary, significantly in Loci 10 and 12 (Connah 1986c: 54, 59, 86, 102, 168, 214). Two cowry shells provided rare evidence of contact with the coast, one a fragment of a big specimen from Locus 10 (Connah 1986c: 62), and the other a very small example from Locus 11 (Connah 1986c: 238). A large fragment of Meroitic window-grill in sandstone was found in unstratified rubble, when clearing part of an adjacent old excavation spoil dump to make Site 1037 accessible for excavation (Connah 1986c: 6). A bronze seal was found in the area west of the terrace wall bordering Locus 12, an area outside of Site 1037 that is not detailed in this book. Peter French thought that this was a Christian seal with a Greek or Coptic monogram (Connah 1986c: 87).

Most personal of the evidence not recorded on the Artefact Index Cards or otherwise available to the authors were the occurrences of what appeared to be human hair. This was found in Locus 5: 'a bit' (Connah 1986c: 66); Locus 8: 'a lot' (Connah 1986c: 70); Locus 10 (Connah 1986c: 62); and Locus 12: 'a curly "lock" of black hair' (Connah 1986c: 54). It also came from Locus 10: 'light brown' (Connah 1986c: 136); and Locus 12: 'handful of' (Connah 1986c: 97). Analysts might now be able to examine its DNA to confirm its human origin and to determine the relationships or otherwise of the individuals from whom it came. Less certain were more frequent occurrences of hair that was only possibly human: Locus 1 (Connah 1986c: 41, 45); Locus 4 (Connah 1986c: 163, 171, 178); Locus 10 (Connah 1986c: 91, 96, 116, 129, 169, 203); and Locus 12 (Connah 1986c: 109, 116, 136). It should be noted that Adams and Adams (2010: 309) recorded a 'cut-off braid' of 'human hair' (78.3.15/8) from a Classic Christian 1 context in House 196 at Qasr Ibrim but this was a little later in date than Site 1037.

8

Faunal and Botanical Evidence from the 1986 Excavation of House 1037

Peter Rowley-Conwy, the bioarchaeologist at Qasr Ibrim, provided faunal and botanical identifications of excavated specimens from Site 1037 in February 1986. His table of identified fauna is reproduced here in a revised form (Table 3), to which is added his botanical identifications from the excavator's field notes (Connah 1986c).

Amongst the organic evidence recovered from Locus 12 there was a range of faunal and botanical remains. This included bread wheat, barley, date stones, castor-oil seeds, fig and halfa grass. Except for the bread wheat, these were from Level 1 (and other contexts: see Table 3) that, as mentioned above, was dated by its pottery content to M2, AD200–350, and by a radiocarbon date (on wood) of cal AD130–531 (Table 1). Other loci at Site 1037 had less botanical material but produced doum palm nuts and the only evidence for grapes. In addition, botanical remains from elsewhere at Qasr Ibrim for the period AD0–550 provided evidence for the 'Islamic' agricultural revolution, during which a range of 'summer' crops including sorghum, cotton, durum wheat, bread wheat, bulrush millet, termis bean and sesame were introduced, at about the time that the *saqia*, the ox-driven waterwheel, was being adopted in the area (Rowley-Conwy 1989; 1991; Fuller 2014).

The midden (Locus 12) also contained bones of cattle and sheep/goat, as well as fish and possibly hartebeest. However, in addition to the same faunal evidence as in Locus 12, there were bones of pig, gazelle, camel, donkey, and dog in other loci. Of these, the camel is known from other evidence to have been present at Qasr Ibrim since sometime in the first millennium BC, much earlier than previously thought (Rowley-Conwy 1988).

Table 3: Analysis of House 1037 faunal and botanical evidence (on-site identifications by Peter Rowley-Conwy)

Locus	Level	Location	Cow	Sheep/Goat	Pig	Other	Botanical
2 (room)	0–40cm	Below EC floor level	0	8 (3sh)	0	0	
2 (room)	0–40cm	Test-pit	3	1	0	0	
2 (room)	40–80cm	Test-pit	2	0	0	0	
2 (room W)	0–30cm	Pit 1 contents	0	0	1	1 (gazelle)	
2 (room W)	0–30cm		14	9 (4sh)	10	0	
2 (room W)	30–60cm		18	8 (1sh, 1gt)	14	0	DPM nut

Locus	Level	Location	Cow	Sheep/Goat	Pig	Other	Botanical
2 (room W)	60–90cm		23	11 (2sh, 1gt, 1 ibex?)	19	0	DPM nuts
2 (room W)	90–120cm		10	10 (1sh)	5	0	
3 (room)	0–40cm	Area of room	7	5 (1sh, 1gt)	0	0	
3 (room E)		Removal of crypts	4	0	1	1 (camel)	
3 (room W)	40–80cm		3	3	0	0	
4 (room)		Lower Fill 1	4	1	0	1 (gazelle)	
4 (room)	Pit 1	Fill	1	2 (1gt)	0	0	
4 (room SW)		Rubble & fill	2	0	0	0	
5 (room NW)	0–20cm		0	1	1	0	
5 (room NW)	80–110cm	And central W	0	0	1	0	
6 (room E)	0–30cm		1	0	0		DPM nut
6 (room E)	30–60cm		0	0	0	2 (gazelle)	
6 (room E)	60–90cm		1	0	0	0	
7 (room E)	0–40cm		13	0	0	1 (donkey)	
8? (room)	0–30cm	Fill	3	1 (1gt)	0	0	
8 (room W)	Fill to 30cm	Below top of stonework	1	0	0	0	
9 (room)		Fill at W end	1	0	0	0	DS
9 (room)		Basal rubble and fill, N side	1	0	1	0	
9 (room N)	0–40cm		1	0	0	1 (donkey)	
10 (room)	0–40cm	Below top N wall	2	0	0	2 (gazelle)	
10 (room)	40–80cm	Below top N wall, room fill					DPM nut, DS, GP
10 (room)	80–120cm	Below top N wall, room fill					DPM nut
10 (room)	120–160cm	Below top N wall	6	0	0	0	
10 (room W)	0–40cm	Area W of Room 10	12	6 (2sh)	0	2 (gazelle)	
10 (room W)	40–80cm	Area W of Room 10	18	2	0	0	DS
10 (room)	75cm–2m	Test-pit	0	1 (1gt)	0	0	
10 (room)	2m–bedrock	Test-pit	3	3 (1sh)	0	1 (fish)	
11 (room W)		Upper fill and unstratified	2	2 (1sh)	0	1 (dog)	
12 (area)	Level 1	Carbonized material & soil	48	1	0	0	B, DS, COS, F, HG
12 (area)	Level 2	Foundation trench fill, terrace wall	2	1	0	0	
12 (area)	Level 5	Fill of N feature	1	0	0	0	
12 (area)	Level 6	Fill of N feature, E part					HG
12 (area)	Level 7	Mudbrick wall & fill E of S feature	2	0	0	0	
12 (area)	0–40cm	Area	8	0	0	1 (hartebeest?) 1 (fish)	DS, BW, COS
12 (area)	Below 40cm	Cleaning surface	1	0	0	1 (hartebeest?)	DS
Totals			**218**	**76**	**53**	**16**	
			363 bones identified				

DPM=Doum palm; DS=Date stones; GP=Grape pips; B=Barley; BW=Bread wheat; COS=Castor-oil seeds; F=Fig; HG=Halfa grass.

9

Discussion and Conclusion

Every archaeological excavation is an experiment, an attempt to learn about the life of people who did not or could not record it themselves. Unfortunately, unlike many scientific experiments, it is one that can never be replicated; the physical evidence of deposits, structures and artefacts can only be fully understood at the time of its disturbance. For this reason the dissemination of the results of an excavation by published means, whether printed, digital, video or other, is essential. If not published, an archaeological excavation becomes merely destruction of a part of the human past, and often an expensive one in time, effort and money. This is particularly so at a site like Qasr Ibrim that is suffering from persistent damage, in this case from the fluctuating water level of Lake Nasser. A time could come when there is little or nothing left for future investigators.

The excavation reported in this book was small but it was intended to be. On an urban site where much of the work before 1986 had consisted of extensive areal investigation, Site 1037 was intended to be intensive and, so far as possible, unlimited by time constraints: a microcosmic examination of life at Qasr Ibrim during the earlier part of the first millennium AD. The excavated structural remains were unimpressive remnants of mud and stone walls and other features, containing mainly fragmentary artefacts that had been discarded or lost. Nevertheless, the two main aims of the project were accomplished; first to test the cultural continuity of a domestic occupation that had lasted for six or seven centuries and was apparently unbroken through the Meroitic, X-Group (Ballaña) and Early Christian periods. The second aim was to provide a window into the lives of the occupants of just one house during this long period.

The first aim was met by the structural sequence that was established for the excavated building. It had been modified many times, often in only minor ways, but resulting in an overall complexity of which parts were difficult to understand. Apparently, there was no occupational hiatus at Site 1037, no attempt to tear everything down and rebuild from scratch. People continued to occupy a structure that was subjected to many alterations over several centuries. Their pottery changed, so that archaeologists have been able to arrange it and other associated artefacts into a relative chronological sequence based on evidence from other Nubian sites. However, absolute chronology remains elusive in the case of Site 1037 because of the difficulty of relating the contents of loci to the structure of the building itself and its modifications. Nevertheless, the site provided evidence of residential continuity in spite of cultural change, so that domestic life in this small urban community, high above the River Nile, probably continued much as before, notwithstanding a shift in religious belief as Christianity was adopted, although some pre-Christian cults could have persisted in domestic contexts (Dijkstra 2013: 114). Evidence of the adoption of Christianity is the deliberate erasure of Meroitic religious symbols from the possibly recycled stone lintel found in Locus 10, at the doorway of what must have become a Christian household. This was presumably done because of the pagan associations of the symbols, although curiously the Meroitic inscription on the lintel was not damaged, perhaps because of the status it gave to the house. Overall, there was little evidence of the cultural and chronological boundaries that have characterized the archaeology of Nubia during the time that 1037 was occupied. Findings from Site 1037 support the conclusion of W.Y. Adams in Adams and Adams (2013: 157):

> The Ballaña period may in sum be regarded as a prolonged transition during which new traditions came piecemeal to replace old ones—the two often existing side by side in a somewhat incongruous combination. As a blend of the old and the new, the culture established no distinctive canons of its own except in the domain of funerary ritual.

The artefactual and ecofactual evidence from the site met the second aim of the excavation. Work for many years on different parts of Qasr Ibrim have produced a rich and diverse collection of such evidence that provides a detailed picture of life at the site as a whole during its many centuries of occupation (Adams and Adams 2010; 2013). In contrast, Site 1037 gave an opportunity to investigate the character of life within just one house. Its occupants lived in a building of stone and mud walls, in which some doorways had dressed stone jambs. Inner surfaces of these walls were plastered with mud and whitewashed and floors were of hard mud. The inhabitants dug crypts (storage pits) beneath the house floors, perhaps to store valuables or grain or to keep food cool during periods of high temperatures. The house might have had an upper floor or have been built at different levels on the sloping site. Some of the building's doors could have had locks, suggesting that security was at times a concern. During the course of the house's occupation there were two possible latrines. There was a range of pottery, including items for water-storage and food preparation and serving. There was also culinary glassware, probably imported from further north. Occupants had a cereal-based diet that included meat from domesticated cattle, sheep/goats, pigs, and a few wild animals and fish. Imported wine was probably available but might also have been made locally. There is evidence of metalworking skills, in copper/bronze, iron, and lead, or at least access to other people with such skills. The inscribed lintel and the ostraka in several languages, suggest the existence of at least limited literacy. Pottery figurines and carvings in wood and ivory indicate the significance of symbolism and art for those living in the house. Baskets, similar to those employed in the 1986 excavation to remove spoil, were in use, rope of high quality was present. Both spinning and weaving were carried on in the house by some of its occupants, who also probably made their own clothing, some of which was decorated with embroidery. Glass and faience beads were worn and cosmetic instruments were in use. There was wooden furniture within the house and at night oil lamps provided light. Arrowheads suggest a capacity for defence. Coinage, probably from elsewhere, might have been in very limited use. Castor-oil pods could have been for medicinal use but might have been to provide oil for the lamps. Indeed, Herodotus, writing about Egypt in the fifth century BC, recorded its use for that purpose, although it gave 'a noisome odour' (Powell 1949: 151).

This was not a high-status household. There was an apparent absence of the high quality painted pottery that is a characteristic of the Meroitic period and virtually no personal items of precious materials were recovered from the site. The only exceptions consisted of minor decoration in gold on two wooden spindle whorls from Locus 8 (86.1.7/39), on a glass or faience bead/amulet from Locus 10 (86.2.5/20), and on a glass bead from Locus 10 (86.2.6/1). Fragmentary though much of the evidence is, it suggests that those living in Site 1037 were people of modest means who had a complex material culture and, secure in their hilltop city, had a relatively safe and comfortable existence by the standards of their times.

In any one lifetime, the people in the 1037 house might not have been unduly concerned that their culture was changing. It is archaeologists not they who distinguished cultural differences by creating the labels that we now use. Perhaps we should reconsider this process and give more attention to detailed vertical excavation contexts and less to generalized horizontal plans. As Smith (2013: 273) commented, citing Emberling (1997), 'The first thing to do is to abandon the search for the chimera of neatly bounded ethnic groups corresponding to a particular material culture assemblage, a common trope in Near Eastern archaeology that is sometimes still uncritically applied today'. The passage of time between the 1986 Qasr Ibrim excavation and the writing of this book has provided an opportunity to re-examine this matter in the light of the evidence from Site 1037.

Finally, the overall significance of Qasr Ibrim in the context of African archaeology and that of wider regions needs to be emphasized. The book edited by van der Vliet and Hagen (2013) is titled *Qasr Ibrim, between Egypt and Africa: studies in cultural exchange,* perhaps implying that neither Egypt nor Qasr Ibrim are part of Africa although no doubt intending to stress the link between the two that the site provides. Both historical and archaeological evidence indicate that the place was of great importance. Historically, the Romans must have thought so when they occupied it in 23 BC (N.K. Adams 2013: 65), making it part of their southernmost extension into Africa and significantly calling it 'Primis', meaning 'First'. Archaeologically, its importance is because of the great amount and diversity of evidence preserved at the site, including writing in a range of languages. As Adams (2013: 46) has commented, in a world context this 'is not wholly unique'. However, he goes on to say: 'But no site yet excavated has yielded anything like the sheer variety of material found at Qasr Ibrim, giving information about every aspect of day-to-day life in a bustling community'. Compared with the majority of archaeological sites in Africa, where excavated evidence is often limited to broken pottery and other inorganic materials, the Qasr Ibrim evidence is really exceptional. For periods later than those with which this book is concerned, the most outstanding is the great variety of textual material but for Qasr Ibrim overall it is the extraordinary amount of textiles that have been recovered and the light that they shed on the site and the world to which it belonged which is important. As Nettie Adams has written: 'The presence of luxury textiles imported from so many different parts of the world, over a period of some 2,000 years indicates the economic and political power held by the inhabitants of Qasr Ibrim. Although the cultural affiliations of the population varied through the centuries, Qasr Ibrim, situated between Egypt and Africa, was ideally positioned to extend its influence and power to the Mediterranean world and beyond' (N.K. Adams 2013a: 81). In this context, archaeological data concerning this site, although 1037 was excavated so long ago, deserves to be resurrected.

References

Adams, N.K. 1986. Textile finds at Qasr Ibrim, 1986. 'Archaeological Textiles Newsletter' 3, 8 and 10.

Adams, N.K. 2013a. Influences from abroad: the evidence from the textiles. In J. van der Vliet and J.L. Hagen (eds), 'Qasr Ibrim, between Egypt and Africa: studies in cultural exchange', 65–81. Leiden, Nederlands Instituut voor het Nabije Oosten.

Adams, N.K. 2013b. Textile material and weaves; dress and ornamentation. In W.Y. Adams and N.K. Adams, 'Qasr Ibrim: the Ballaña Phase', 107–17. London, Egypt Exploration Society, Excavation Memoir 104.

Adams, W.Y. 1977. 'Nubia: corridor to Africa'. London, Allen Lane.

Adams, W.Y. 1982. Qasr Ibrim: an archaeological conspectus. In 'Nubian studies: Proceedings of the Symposium for Nubian Studies, Selwyn College, Cambridge, 1978', J.M. Plumley (ed.), 25–33. Warminster, England, International Society for Nubian Studies, Aris & Phillips.

Adams, W.Y. 1984. 'Nubia: corridor to Africa'. London, Allen Lane. (Reprinted 1984.) Adams, W.Y. 1986. 'Ceramic industries of medieval Nubia', Parts I and II. Lexington, University Press of Kentucky.

Adams, W.Y. 1993. Medieval Nubia: another Golden Age. 'Expedition', 35(2), 28–39. Adams, W.Y. 1996. 'Qasr Ibrim: the Late Mediaeval period'. London, Egypt Exploration Society, Excavation Memoir 59.

Adams, W.Y. 2000. 'Meinarti I: The Late Meroitic, Ballaña and Transitional Occupation'. Oxford, British Archaeological Reports International Series 895, BAR Publishing.

Adams, W.Y. 2013. Qasr Ibrim: connecting the dots. In J. van der Vliet and J.L. Hagen (eds), 'Qasr Ibrim, between Egypt and Africa: studies in cultural exchange', 45–63. Leiden, Nederlands Instituut voor het Nabije Oosten.

Adams, W.Y. and Adams, N.K. 2010. 'Qasr Ibrim: the Earlier Medieval period'. London, Egypt Exploration Society, Excavation Memoir 89.

Adams, W.Y. and Adams, N.K. 2013. 'Qasr Ibrim: the Ballaña Phase'. London, Egypt Exploration Society, Excavation Memoir 104.

Alexander, J. 1984a. Preliminary Report to the Egypt Exploration Society: Qasr Ibrim 1984. Unpublished typescript. Egypt Exploration Society Expedition to Ibrim March 1984.

Alexander, J. 1984b. Notes on the Eastern Terraces. Qasr Ibrim unpublished field records archived in the British Museum, London.

Alexander, J. 1987. The 1986 Excavations at Qasr Ibrim. Unpublished Report, E.E.S. Qasr Ibrim Archive.

Alexander, J. 1988. The Saharan divide in the Nile Valley: the evidence from Qasr Ibrim. 'African Archaeological Review' 6, 73–90.

Alexander, J. 1999. A new hilltop cemetery and temple of the Meroitic and Post-Meroitic period at Qasr Ibrim. 'Sudan and Nubia' 3, 47–59, Plates XXVI–XXVIII.

Alexander, J.A. and Driskell, B. 1985. Qasr Ibrim 1984. 'Journal of Egyptian Archaeology' 71, 12–26, Plate II.

Alexander, J.A., Driskell, B. and Connah, G. in press. Qasr Ibrim 1986. 'Journal of Egyptian Archaeology' 74, never published.

Anderson, R.D. and Adams, W.Y. 1979. Qasr Ibrim 1978. 'Journal of Egyptian Archaeology' 65, 30–41.

Connah, G. 1986a. Unpublished typescript entitled: Area 4: The Southeast Terraces [Qasr Ibrim excavation Site 1037], revised to 31 October 1986 and submitted to John Alexander.

Connah, G. 1986b. Unpublished manuscript about the excavation of Site 1037, February 1986. Submitted to the Egyptian Antiquities Service.

Connah, G. 1986c. 1037 Field Notes (Excavator's Archives).

Connah, G.1987. 'African civilizations: precolonial cities and states in tropical Africa: an archaeological perspective', Cambridge, Cambridge University Press.

Connah, G. 1988. 'Of the hut I builded: the archaeology of Australia's history'. Melbourne, Cambridge University Press.

Connah, G. 1996. 'Kibiro: the salt of Bunyoro, past and present'. London, British Institute in Eastern Africa, Memoir 13.

Connah, G. (ed.) 1998. 'Transformations in Africa: essays on Africa's later past'. London, Leicester University Press (Cassell Academic).

Connah, G. 2001. 'African civilizations: an archaeological perspective'. Second Edition, Cambridge, Cambridge University Press.

Connah, G. 2004. 'Forgotten Africa: an introduction to its archaeology'. London and New York, Routledge. Subsequently published also in German, French, Italian, and Portuguese editions.

Connah, G. 2007. 'The same under a different sky? A country estate in nineteenth-century New South Wales'. Oxford, British Archaeological Reports, International Series 1625.

Connah, G. 2010. 'Writing about archaeology'. New York, Cambridge University Press.

Connah, G. 2016. 'African civilizations: an archaeological perspective'. Third Edition, New York, Cambridge University Press.

Connor, C.L. 1998. 'The color of ivory: polychromy on Byzantine ivories'. Princeton, New Jersey, Princeton University Press.

Dijkstra, J.H.F. 2013. Qasr Ibrim and the religious transformation of Lower Nubia in Late Antiquity. In J. van der Vliet and J.L. Hagen (eds), 'Qasr Ibrim, between Egypt and Africa: studies in cultural exchange', 110–22. Leiden, Nederlands Instituut voor het Nabije Oosten.

Driskell, B.N., Adams, N.K., and French, P.G. 1989. A newly discovered temple at Qasr Ibrim: preliminary report. 'Archéologie du Nil Moyen' 3, 11–54.

Eigner, D. 2013. A stone building in the desert sands: some remarks on the architecture of the Gala Abu Ahmed Fortress. In 'The power of walls: fortifications in ancient northeastern Africa', F. Jesse and C. Vogel (eds), 309–19. Köln, Heinrich-Barth-Institut.

Emberling, G. 1997. Ethnicity in complex societies: archaeological perspectives. 'Journal of Archaeological Research' 5(4), 295–344.

Fuller, D.Q. 2014. Agricultural innovation and state collapse in Meroitic Nubia: the impact of the savannah package. In 'Archaeology of African plant use', C.J. Stevens, S. Nixon, M.A. Murray and D.Q. Fuller (eds), 165–77. Walnut Creek, California, Left Coast Press.

Garstang, J., Sayce, A.H. and Griffiths, F.W. 1911. 'Meroë, the city of the Ethiopians'. Oxford, Oxford University Press.

Geus, F. 1991. Burial customs in the upper main Nile: an overview. In 'Egypt and Africa: Nubia from prehistory to Islam', W.V. Davies (ed.), 57–73. British Museum Press, London.

Hammond, N. 1990. Introduction: Book reviews. 'Journal of Field Archaeology' 17, 471–2.

Horton, M. 1990. Book review of Adams, W.Y. 1986. 'Ceramic industries of medieval Nubia. Memoirs of the UNESCO Archaeological Survey of Sudanese Nubia 1', (2 volumes). Lexington. University of Kentucky Press. 'Journal of Field Archaeology' 17, 485–8.

Horton, M. 1991. Africa in Egypt: new evidence from Qasr Ibrim. In 'Egypt and Africa: Nubia from prehistory to Islam', W.V. Davies (ed.), 264–77. British Museum Press, London.

Leclant, J., Heyler, A., Berger-el Naggar, C., Carrier, C. and Rilly, C. 2000. 'Répertoire D'Épigraphie Méroïtique: corpus des inscriptions publiées'. Tome III REM 1001 À REM 1278. Paris, Académie Des Inscriptions Et Belles-Lettres, Diffusion De Boccard.

Lipka, M. 2009. 'Religions in the Graeco-Roman World'. Volume 167, 'Roman Gods: A Conceptual Approach', Leiden, Boston, Brill.

Mattingly, D.J. (ed) 2013. 'The archaeology of Fazzān', Volume 4, 'Survey and excavations at Old Jarma (Ancient Garama) carried out by C.M. Daniels (1962–69) and the Fazzān Project (1997–2001)'. London, Society for Libyan Studies.

OxCal 2012. OxCal/ORAU/NERC Radiocarbon Facility. https://c14.arch.ox.ac.uk Accessed 24 October 2012.

OxCal 2016. OxCal/ORAU/NERC Radiocarbon Facility. https://c14.arch.ox.ac.uk Accessed 30 March 2016.

Pitt Rivers, Lieutenant-General. 1898. 'Excavations at Cranborne Chase, near Rushmore … 1893–1896', Vol. IV. London, Privately printed.

Plumley, J.M., Adams, W.Y. and Crowfoot, E. 1977. Qasr Ibrim, 1976. 'Journal of Egyptian Archaeology' 63, 29–47.

Powell, J.E. (Translated) 1949. 'Herodotus', Volume I. Oxford, Clarendon Press.

Reisner, G.A. 1910. 'The archaeological survey of Nubia: report for 1907–8'. Volume I, Cairo.

Rose, P. 1998. Excavations at Qasr Ibrim: Qasr Ibrim 1998. 'Sudan and Nubia' 2: 61–4 and Plates XXXVIII–XLIV.

Rose, P. 2000. Excavations at Qasr Ibrim 2000. 'Sudan and Nubia' 4, 2–4.

Rose, P. 2011. Qasr Ibrim: the last 3000 years. 'Sudan and Nubia' 15, 1–9.

Rowley-Conwy, P. 1988. The camel in the Nile Valley: new Radiocarbon Accelerator (AMS) dates from Qasr Ibrim. 'Journal of Egyptian Archaeology' 74, 245–8 and Plate XXXV.

Rowley-Conwy, P. 1989. Nubia AD 0–550 and the 'Islamic' agricultural revolution: preliminary botanical evidence from Qasr Ibrim, Egyptian Nubia. 'Archéologie du Nil Moyen' 3, 131–8.

Rowley-Conwy, P. 1991. Sorghum from Qasr Ibrim, Egyptian Nubia, c.800 BC–AD 1811: a preliminary study. In 'New light on early farming: recent developments in palaeoethnobotany', J.M. Renfrew (ed.), 191–212. Edinburgh, Edinburgh University Press.

Ruffini, G.R. 2012. 'Medieval Nubia: a social and economic history'. Oxford, Oxford University Press.

Shinnie, P.L. 1967. 'Meroe: a civilization of the Sudan'. London, Thames and Hudson.

Smith, S.T. 2013. The garrison and inhabitants: a view from Askut. In 'The power of walls: fortifications in ancient northeastern Africa', F. Jesse and C. Vogel (eds), 269–91. Köln, Heinrich-Barth-Institut.

Török, L. 1997. 'Meroe city: an ancient African capital: John Garstang's excavations in the Sudan, Parts 1 & 2'. London, Egypt Exploration Society.

van der Vliet, J. and Hagen, J.L (eds) 2013, 'Qasr Ibrim, between Egypt and Africa: studies in cultural exchange'. Leiden, Nederlands Instituut voor het Nabije Oosten.

Veldmeijer, A.J. 2013. 'Leatherwork from Qasr Ibrim (Egypt). Part 1: Footwear from the Ottoman Period'. Leiden, Sidestone Press, The Netherlands.

White, J.P. 1983. Report writing and publication. In 'Australian field archaeology: A guide to techniques', G. Connah (ed.), 171–8. Canberra, Australian Institute of Aboriginal Studies.

Żurawski, B. 2013. Strongholds on the Middle Nile: Nubian fortifications of the Middle Ages. In 'The power of walls: fortifications in ancient northeastern Africa', F. Jesse and C. Vogel (eds), 113–43. Köln, Heinrich-Barth-Institut.